GRACE EV[illegible] SOCIETY

"Faith Alone in Christ Alone"

VOLUME 38 AUTUMN 2025 NUMBER 75

Simon and the Sinful Woman: One or Two Believers? (Luke 7:36-50)
Kenneth Yates 3

The Gospel of John: Evangelistic Book, or Something Else?
John Claeys 17

Preparing to Have a Lavish Kingdom Entrance (Part 2)
David Janssen 33

Did They Really Believe? (John 2:23)
Hershall Spradley 45

What Is the Main Point of Ecclesiastes?
Brad Doskocil 57

The Carrot or the Stick? A Neurophysiological and Theological Approach to Sustained Eternal Focus
Ellie Stevens Strathman 67

Eternal Rewards Teaching in the Old Testament
Robert N. Wilkin 85

Book Reviews 99

Journal of the

GRACE EVANGELICAL SOCIETY

Published Semiannually by GES

Editor
Kenneth W. Yates

Associate Editor
Robert N. Wilkin

Layout
Lisa Simpson

Manuscripts, book reviews, and other communications should be addressed to GES, Director of Publications, P.O. Box 1308, Denton, TX 76202 or submissions@faithalone.org.

Journal subscriptions, renewals, and changes of address should be sent to the Grace Evangelical Society, P.O. Box 1308, Denton, TX 76202 or email ges@faithalone.org. Subscription Rates: single copy, $9.25 (U.S.); 1 year, $18.50; 2 years, $35.00; 3 years, $49.50; 4 years, $62.00; $13.50 per year for active full-time students. Please add $4.00 for US shipping. Add $4.50 per year for shipping to Mexico and Canada and $8.50 per year for all other international shipping. New subscriptions, 1 year, $9.25; gift subscriptions, 1 year, $9.25.

Purpose: Grace Evangelical Society was formed "to promote the clear proclamation of God's free salvation through faith alone in Christ alone, which is properly correlated with and distinguished from issues related to discipleship."

We Affirm: God, out of love for the human race, sent the Lord Jesus Christ into the world to save sinners. He paid the full penalty for human sin when He died on the cross. Any person who believes in Jesus Christ for everlasting life receives that gift which, as the words *everlasting life* suggest, can never be lost (John 1:29; 3:16-18; 19:30; 1 Tim 1:16).

Third-class postage has been paid at Dallas, Texas. Postmaster: Send address changes to Grace Evangelical Society, P.O. Box 1308, Denton, TX 76202

PRINTED IN THE UNITED STATES OF AMERICA

ISBN: 978-1-943399-72-7

SIMON AND THE SINFUL WOMAN: ONE OR TWO BELIEVERS? (LUKE 7:36-50)

BY KENNETH YATES

Editor
Journal of the Grace Evangelical Society

I. INTRODUCTION

In Luke 7, we read about a Pharisee named Simon who invites the Lord to his home for a meal. The meal is interrupted by a woman who washes the Lord's feet with her tears and dries them with her hair. Christ uses the situation to teach about the forgiveness of sins and love for Him.

It is common to understand this passage (Luke 7:36-50) in an evangelistic way. Simon is seen as an unbeliever, while the woman is portrayed as a believer. She sees her own sinfulness, but Simon does not see his. She responds to her sin in a God-pleasing way, but Simon does not. She experiences the forgiveness of sins, which results in eternal salvation. Simon is not forgiven of his sins and is therefore spiritually condemned.

In this article, I will argue that both Simon and the woman are believers. The Lord's teaching about the forgiveness of sins is not evangelistic, but intended to instruct believers, one of whom was Simon.

II. THE PASSAGE

Before discussing the highlights of the dinner at Simon's house, it would be helpful to consider the immediate context.

A. The Context (Luke 7:29-35)

Luke records how the people of Israel had responded to the ministry of John the Baptist. Many of the tax collectors and sinners submitted to his baptism. Most of the religious leaders did not (vv 29-30).

The Lord compares the leaders to silly children in the marketplace. It is impossible to please them. They rejected John's preaching because he was a strict ascetic. They rejected Christ's preaching because He was perceived as being too lenient—even eating with sinners. John, in their opinion, had a demon. This was either because John was seen as a lunatic or because demonic activity was associated with the desert, the place of John's ministry.[1] The Pharisees thought Christ was an immoral drunk (vv 31-34).

Christ refers to those who accepted the preaching of John and Christ as wise (v 35). They were not like the foolish, unbelieving religious leaders.

Many fail to distinguish between John's ministry and the ministry of the Lord Jesus. John called people to repentance—to turn from sin. Jesus, on the other hand, offered grace—eternal life through faith in Him. Those who do not recognize that there is a difference between the two messages say that eternal salvation demands both. According to their reasoning, those who believe will demonstrate their faith by the changed life that repentance brings.[2]

It is a common view in Evangelicalism that eternal salvation is granted only after one repents of his sins. This view does not recognize that John's message was specifically for the nation of Israel. The kingdom would not come to that generation of Jews unless the nation as a whole repented. Eternal life, on the other hand, is given by faith alone; repentance is not a requirement. The result of turning from sin is not eternal life, but harmony—fellowship—with God.[3] The nation of Israel was out of fellowship with God.

A person could have heard John's message, yet not have turned from their sin. But if that same person heard Jesus' message and believed in Him for eternal life, that person immediately received eternal life, based on Jesus' unconditional promises.

Luke 7:29-30 are not evangelistic verses. Most of the religious leaders were not believers. It should be noted that while a believer who did not repent of his sin was unwise, he still had eternal life. It is a mistake to equate the foolish with unbelievers and the wise with believers. There were exceptions.

---

[1] Walter L. Liefeld and David W. Pao, "Luke," in *The Expositor's Bible Commentary: Luke–Acts* (Grand Rapids, MI: Zondervan, 2007), 148.

[2] John A. Martin, "Luke," in *The Bible Knowledge Commentary*, eds. J. F. Walvoord and R. B. Zuck (Wheaton, IL: Victor Books, 1985), 223; Robert H. Stein, *Luke*, The New American Commentary (Nashville, TN: Broadman & Holman Publishers, 1992), 233; Warren W. Wiersbe, *The Bible Exposition Commentary* (Wheaton, IL: Victor Books, 1996), 197.

[3] Zane C. Hodges, *Absolutely Free!* (Grand Rapids, MI: Zondervan, 1989), 144-46.

In the following verses, there is a "sinner" and a Pharisee. It should not be assumed, as often happens, that the "sinner" is a believer and the Pharisee an unbeliever. There were some "sinners" who were not believers, and some Pharisees who were believers.

I will argue that the Pharisee Simon and the woman who is a "sinner" are both believers. One, however, is wiser than the other.[4]

B. The Encounter (Luke 7:36-50)

Simon invites Christ to his home for a meal, and the Lord accepts the invitation. Stein suggests that Simon asked the Lord to come to his home because of Jesus' reputation as a prophet.[5] In the eyes of those who have accepted the message of John and Jesus, this gives Simon an exalted status (v 35). Jesus reclines at the table and eats with Simon and the other guests he has invited.

This meal would have been known to the public because Jesus was present. Those who were not invited would have the privilege of sitting outside Simon's home and listening in on the conversations and the Lord's teachings. Luke mentions a particular woman in this outer group.[6]

She is called a "sinner" (v 37), which immediately reminds the reader of the sinners who responded to Christ's preaching and were counted among His friends (vv 29, 34). While many conclude that she was a prostitute, she may have simply been an ordinary Jew who did not keep the strict requirements of the oral law practiced by the Pharisees.[7]

Breaking social decorum, this woman approaches the table where the Lord is reclining with Simon. She washes Jesus' feet with her tears and expensive perfume. She probably wore this perfume around her neck. By touching Him, she breaks religious taboos. By letting down her hair to dry His feet, she publicly disgraces herself.[8] Her actions towards Him were costly and required great humility.[9]

---

[4] Alberto S. Valdés, "Luke," in *The Grace New Testament Commentary*, ed. Robert N. Wilkin (Denton, TX: Grace Evangelical Society, 2019), 132.

[5] Stein, *Luke,* 236.

[6] Martin, "Luke," 224.

[7] Leon Morris, *The Gospel According to St. Luke* (Grand Rapids, MI: Eerdmans, 1974), 146.

[8] Stein, *Luke,* 236.

[9] R. C. Sproul, *A Walk with God: An Exposition of Luke* (Great Britain: Christian Focus Publications, 1999), 152.

Simon's thoughts express the woman's failure to observe the norms of decorum. He is surprised that she would behave this way, but more surprised that Jesus would allow it. Many of the "sinners" had concluded that Jesus was a prophet (vv 16-17), but Simon reasons that this cannot be the case; if He were a prophet, He would not allow such a sinful woman to touch Him, making Him ceremonially unclean.

The Lord can read Simon's thoughts. This leads to a parable in which the Lord describes two debtors. One owes a lender ten times more than the other, but the lender forgives both their debts. Christ asks Simon which of the debtors will love the lender more. Simon correctly answers that the one who was forgiven the most will love the most.

Christ explains that the woman is the one who has been forgiven much. As a result, she loves much. Simon is the one who has been forgiven little and thus loves little. This is seen in their actions. The woman went to great lengths to show her love for the Lord by washing His feet with her tears and anointing them with expensive ointment. She greeted Him with profound respect. Simon, on the other hand, did not. He did not wash the Lord's feet with water when He came to his house, nor anoint His head with cheap, common oil. These were customs that a host would typically perform for an invited guest.

Many point out that Simon was not being rude to the Lord, since such acts of courtesy were not mandatory for a host. But they were seen as kind gestures. The point is that the woman went far above what was required, while Simon did not see the need to put forth any special effort to welcome the Lord.[10] She showed her great love, while Simon showed a small amount of love.

The Lord concludes that the reason the woman loved much was because she had been forgiven much. All agree that in the parable, the person with the larger debt represents the woman, while Simon is the other debtor.

With these words, the Lord told the woman to go in *peace*. Her faith had *saved* her.

---

[10] I. H. Marshall, *The Gospel of Luke* (Grand Rapids, MI: Eerdmans, 1978), 312-13; Liefeld and Pao, "Luke," 151; Stein, *Luke*, 237.

III. IS THIS ABOUT THE WOMAN'S ETERNAL SALVATION?

All agree that the sinful woman was a believer. She had eternal life. Many argue that the whole episode describes how she obtained eternal life. They point to various aspects of the account. The following paragraphs trace their faulty reasoning.

A. The Context

Many tax collectors believed in the preaching of both John and Jesus (v 29). They, and sinners who were associated with them, were called *friends* of the Lord (v 34). This woman is called a sinner (v 37). Pharisees, rather than sinners, are used as illustrations of unbelievers. Those who respond to John's and Jesus' preaching, including turning from their sins, are saved from the lake of fire. Those who don't respond are spiritually condemned. This sinful woman responds well, as seen by the Lord's commendation of her.

B. She Repented

Since John called for the nation to repent, the sinner who believed him needed to turn from his sin. This woman does that. The humility she shows towards the Lord reveals her repentance. The whole episode is said to show her as a "penitent" whose demeanor is what the Lord demands of "repentant sinners." This is necessary for their obtaining salvation. Grace and justification are given to the one who is humble.[11]

Stein agrees and says that this woman knew she was a sinner and needed to repent. John and Jesus offered forgiveness, and she accepted it gladly.[12] Her tears should be understood as tears of remorse over her sin.[13]

Wiersbe says the woman was saved from hell because she repented of her sins and put her faith in Christ. The love she expressed in her tears and the use of the expensive ointment were proof of that salvation. It resulted in the peace in which the Lord told her to go.[14]

---

[11] John Peter Lange and J. J. van Oosterzee, *A Commentary on the Holy Scriptures: Luke*, trans. Philip Schaff and Charles C. Starbuck (Bellingham, WA: Logos Bible Software, 2008), 124.

[12] Stein, *Luke*, 233.

[13] Liefeld and David W. Pao, "Luke," 150.

[14] Wiersbe, *The Bible Exposition Commentary*, 199.

C. Forgiveness of Sins

Forgiveness of sins is often seen as being synonymous with receiving eternal life. Wiersbe sees forgiveness as a gift of God's grace. When this woman was forgiven, she accepted God's free offer of eternal salvation. Stein says the forgiveness of sins in this account is a metaphor for being saved from the lake of fire.[15]

D. Her Works Proved She Was Saved

Reformed theologians point to the woman's works. These works are said to portray the reality of her faith. By approaching the Lord in that setting and letting her hair down in public in order to serve Him, she showed her willingness to suffer ridicule for her faith. Even though she was not wealthy, she paid the price for the perfume in order to please Him. Her actions showed that she did not have an intellectual faith, which cannot save, but a true faith that manifests itself in godly deeds. Only that kind of faith saves.

Wiersbe says that her works showed she had a faith that expressed itself through love. Without those works, her faith would have been dead (Jas 2:14-26; Gal 5:6). Jesus accepted her tears and the perfume because her works were evidence of her faith.[16] Stein agrees and adds that the love she had for the Lord was evidence that she had believed. Only when Jesus saw that evidence could He state that her sins were forgiven.[17] That is how He knew she had truly believed.

E. Conclusion

Some see the account of the sinful woman in Simon's home as a discussion on how an unbeliever comes to faith. She is an example of what is required in order to obtain eternal life. She believes in Christ, but it is a repentant faith that is willing to turn from its sinful ways. She recognizes that she is a sinner who needs forgiveness, and she feels deep remorse for her sins.

She also shows that true faith is not sterile. It is public and is willing to pay whatever price is required. Even though salvation is free, the faith that procures it must manifest itself in good works and love for

---

[15] Ibid., 198; Stein, *Luke,* 238.

[16] Wiersbe, *The Bible Exposition Commentary*, 198.

[17] Stein, *Luke,* 237.

the Lord. True faith is costly. *Forgiveness of sins* and *peace with God* are other ways to express being saved from the lake of fire.

IV. WHAT ABOUT SIMON?

Those who view the sinful woman as an illustration of a new believer tend to view Simon as an unbeliever. Many details in the account are said to show that he did not believe in Jesus for eternal life.

A. Context

In the immediate context, Pharisees are silly children who are unbelievers and do not respond to the Lord or to John. Simon, a Pharisee, is an example of such a silly child.

B. He Does Not Repent

There are no tears of repentance from Simon. As a Pharisee, he does not see the need to repent. Unlike the woman, who knows the depth of her sin, he does not see his sin. In his mind, others need to repent, but not a righteous Pharisee. Those who see Simon as an unbeliever say that without repenting, he could not have received eternal salvation.[18]

In this view, the parable of the two debtors does not deal with the amount of actual sin in an individual's life. Since Simon is an unbeliever, he did not receive the forgiveness of a small amount of sin; he did not receive *any* forgiveness at all. The parable speaks of the *awareness* of sin. Simon was just as great a sinner as the woman, but did not realize it.

C. There Is No Statement about the Forgiveness of His Sins

Jesus says the woman's sins are forgiven, but there is no such pronouncement regarding Simon. Christ says the woman can go in peace, but He does not say this to Simon.

D. His Works Prove That He Was Not Saved

Simon does no good works that show his love for the Lord. He doesn't extend common courtesy to Him as a guest by washing His feet or anointing His head. He disrespects Him by concluding that He is not a prophet, even though the common people believe Him to be. He calls Him by the fairly common title of "teacher."

---

[18] Ibid., 233.

One writer says that the Lord makes it clear that the one who is forgiven much, loves much. Therefore, if a man believes he has been forgiven, love for the Lord surely follows. If one does not have forgiveness of sins, there is no love.[19]

Since he is seen as an unbeliever, many question Simon's reason for inviting the Lord to his home in the first place. In fact, some claim that the invitation is further evidence of Simon's lack of good works. Without explaining how he knows Simon's mental attitude, Lange says that the Pharisee only "grudgingly" asked the Lord to dinner.[20] Martin suggests that Simon wanted to "trick" the Lord in some way.[21] Sproul says that since Simon was "obviously" not a believer, he only invited Jesus to his home so he would have the opportunity to trap or interrogate Him.[22] These all portray the dinner at Simon's house as an opportunity to make the Lord look foolish, similar to what the religious leaders do in the temple in Mark 11:27–12:27.

Reformed theology asserts that genuine faith will lead to pure motives and good deeds. Simon had neither.

E. Conclusion

Most writers consider Simon an unbeliever for two reasons. The first is what he does and does not do. He shows no love for the Lord and treats Him rudely. He shows no remorse for his sins. Even worse, it appears that he is not aware of his need for forgiveness. Without the knowledge of, and repentance for, sins, the unbeliever cannot be saved.

The other reason is the context. The Pharisees are opposed to Christ, and Simon is part of that group. Earlier, the Pharisees were those who refused to listen to the Lord's teachings. Christ accepts Simon's invitation because He is reaching out to an unbeliever who needs eternal life. He hopes that Simon will be more open to what He has to say if He speaks to him in the comfort of his own home. Jesus sees it as an evangelistic opportunity in which an enemy might come to repentant faith.[23]

---

[19] Lange and Oosterzee, *Luke,* 124.

[20] Ibid., 123-24.

[21] Martin, "Luke," 223.

[22] Sproul, *A Walk with God,* 154.

[23] Lange and Oosterzee, *Luke,* 124.

V. SIMON IS A BELIEVER

Often, those who claim that Simon was an unbeliever also proclaim that eternal salvation is by grace through faith alone. However, they argue that Simon was not a believer because he did not exhibit good works by repenting of his sins and loving the Lord the way the sinful woman did. This is the contradiction in which Reformed or Calvinistic theology finds itself.

If Simon were an unbeliever, that could not be determined by his rudeness and lack of tears. It would be due only to his lack of faith in Christ as the One who gives eternal life as a free gift.

All the evidence in this account suggests that Simon was a believer.

A. Context

Many Pharisees rejected God's will (v 30). However, though the majority of them were unbelievers, it does not necessarily follow that all who rejected God's will were unbelievers. Luke says that these religious leaders rejected God's will in that they had not been baptized by John. A Pharisee could have believed that Jesus was the Christ, but for fear of what the Jews would do to him, he did not publicly undergo John's baptism (John 12:42-43).

A Pharisee could also have believed in Jesus but had rejected God's will regarding his need to repent of his sins. John the Baptist and Jesus both preached repentance, but turning from sins is not required of the unbeliever in order to obtain eternal life. Repentance and faith are separate issues.

During Christ's ministry, there were different views among believers regarding the need for repentance, just as there are among believers today. Some would have taken seriously what John and Jesus said about repentance. Some would have been lukewarm about the need for it. Still others would not have seen any need to repent. The sinful woman and Simon viewed the seriousness of their sins in different ways. Believers in every age demonstrate various levels of maturity.

Luke sets Simon apart from the Pharisees described in vv 29-33. They said that John had a demon and Jesus was a drunkard. Simon, on the other hand, invites Jesus to his home for a meal. It is not likely that a religiously righteous Jew like Simon would invite a drunk, or a man he thought to be associated with demons, to eat with him.

While it does not prove that Simon was a believer, it is noteworthy that Luke knows his name. Luke interviewed many people when he wrote his Gospel (Luke 1:1-4). If Simon were an unbeliever who wanted to make the Lord look like a fool but failed, it is not likely that the believers who told Luke what happened would remember Simon's name twenty-five years later. It is very possible that these early believers remembered Simon's name because he was one of them.

Jesus teaches Simon, using the woman as an illustration. The Lord's teachings in Simon's home were not evangelistic in nature. They focus, instead, on loving the Lord and thus contain discipleship truths. If Simon were an unbeliever and the Lord had come to his home in hopes of seeing him saved from the lake of fire, He would have preached the gospel of eternal life to him. That is what He did with the unbelieving Pharisee, Nicodemus, in John 3:3-16.

In v 35, immediately before we are introduced to Simon, the Lord mentions wise *children*. The evidence strongly suggests that Simon was one of Christ's children. The woman was, too. Surprisingly, she was wiser than the self-righteous Pharisee.[24]

B. Simon Receives the Forgiveness of Sins

In the parable the Lord taught in Simon's house, Simon is the debtor who is forgiven little. As a result, he loves little. Those who maintain that Simon was an unbeliever say he was not forgiven at all. In what is clearly eisegesis, they say that to be *forgiven little* means that one is *unaware* of his sin. If you are unaware of your sin, you remain unforgiven.[25]

We should follow the plain meaning of the Lord's words. Simon was forgiven. He was forgiven for fewer sins than the woman. One option is that he did not realize the extent of his sins. In his mind, the Lord had forgiven him of relatively few sins.

The other option is that Simon actually had fewer sins for which he was forgiven. Since this woman was well-known for her sinful lifestyle and was possibly a prostitute, she may very well have had a longer list of sins than a proud and self-righteous religious leader. The Lord acknowledged that her sins were *many* (v 40).

---

[24] Valdés, "Luke," 132.

[25] Wiersbe, *The Bible Exposition Commentary*, 198.

Simon believed that Jesus was the Christ (John 20:30-31). He had eternal life. He was forgiven, even if he thought he had few sins for which he needed forgiveness.

C. Simon's Actions

While Simon's actions were probably rude, and the product of a prideful heart, such actions do not mean he didn't believe. A believer can be arrogant. As such a believer, Simon felt that the Christ would value time spent with him. He was a religious Jew who thought that the King would be impressed with him. If the Lord were going to praise somebody at the dinner, Simon thought it would have been him and not the sinful woman. Simon clearly did not see the need to go out of his way to welcome Christ into his home. He was a believer who had an inflated opinion of himself.

The Calvinist often argues that Simon was not a believer because he did not love the Lord. If he had loved Him, he would have washed His feet and anointed His head. But the Lord's parable indicates that Simon *did* love the Lord. But he loved Him *little.*

When Simon called Jesus "Teacher," it did not indicate that he did not believe He was the Christ. Nathanael believes that Jesus is the Christ, but addresses Him as "Rabbi," which is another word for *teacher* (John 1:49). Bartimaeus is another believer who calls Him by that title (Mark 10:51).[26] Mary Magdalene does as well, when she recognizes Him after His resurrection (John 20:16). Simon acknowledges that Jesus is an authoritative teacher even though He was not trained in the Rabbinic schools. Simon is not like the majority of Pharisees, who saw Christ as a drunk and someone to be rejected (v 34).

The NT says that Christ is our King, Priest, and Prophet, thus fulfilling the main offices found in the OT. Very few believers in the NT understood that Jesus was their priest. Among those who believed in Him as the Christ, there were differing views about His role as a prophet. Simon's unspoken doubts about Jesus' being a prophet do not exclude him from believing that He was the Christ. Many have come to faith without believing or understanding that Jesus is our Great High Priest as well as our Prophet.

---

[26] Ken Yates, *Mark: Lessons in Discipleship* (Denton, TX: Grace Evangelical Society, 2025), 403-405.

VI. THE WOMAN WAS ALREADY A BELIEVER

While it is common to see the Lord's encounter with the sinful woman as evangelistic, it is not. The woman was already a believer. The Lord's words about her deal with realities after one receives eternal life. They are discipleship truths. Her actions are those of a wise believer.

Before the encounter, Luke relates that sinners were often friends of Christ. They listened to both His and John's messages. As they listened, many of them believed in Him.

This woman is one of those "sinners." She wants to be close to Him and serve Him. As a believer, she comes prepared to do so, carrying her expensive ointment.

Her tears were likely not tears of remorse over her many sins.[27] They were more likely tears of gratitude for the life He had given her and the privilege of being with Him. The ointment was an expression of that gratitude. The ointment did not prove that her faith was real. She wanted to serve Him, and no price was too high.

Being forgiven of sins is not the same thing as receiving eternal life. In Acts 2:38, believing Jews—who already have eternal life because of their belief—receive the forgiveness of sins after they are baptized. The forgiveness of sins brings fellowship with the Lord (1 John 1:9).[28] When the Lord said this woman's sins were forgiven, that was in addition to her having already received eternal life. She could have communion with the King. She could be close to Him, even though her many sins had wrecked her life. Nothing she had done would prevent her from sitting at His feet.

Simon was amazed that the Christ would allow such a woman to touch Him. He felt that the Christ would only want people like himself to be close to Him. But Jesus says that the woman has full access to Him.

Unbelievers cannot love the Lord. But believers can. This woman loved Him for all He had done for her.

The woman's gratitude and love for the Lord were on full display. Her faith, not tears of remorse, had saved her. She did not have to pour out expensive perfume to prove her faith. That faith had given her eternal life, but it gave her more. It brought the forgiveness of sins

---

[27] Martin, "Luke," 224.

[28] Zane C. Hodges, *The Gospel Under Siege* (Dallas, TX: Redención Viva, 1981), 118. Yates, *Mark,* 78-79.

and allowed someone like her to sit at the feet of the King. Her sins had made it impossible to have communion with Him. Now, she had peace with Him.

VII. CONCLUSION

People often turn to the Synoptic Gospels to find clear gospel presentations for those who are not believers. But these books were written to believers. Luke is no exception. It was written to Theophilus, who was a Christian (Luke 1:4). It is not an evangelistic book.

It should not surprise us, then, that the account of Simon and the sinful woman does not show an unbeliever how to receive eternal life. Instead, it tells us how, as believers, we receive more than eternal life when we believe in Christ. We also receive the forgiveness of sins. Forgiveness allows us to approach the Lord, love Him, and draw closer to Him.

Eating a meal with someone is a picture of fellowship. Simon does that with the Lord. He was a believer, but did not realize how much mercy had been extended in order for him to have eternal life, as well as the privilege of communing with the Lord. His pride led him to believe that it was only natural for him to eat with the King. He was a Law-observing, religious Pharisee. The King would certainly want to be with believers like him.

The woman did not have that attitude. Since believing in Him, she had come to realize that He wanted to eat with her. How could that be? She understood perfectly well the greatness of His mercy in forgiving all her sins. She came to that dinner to express her gratitude.

Simon knew that it was a privilege to have Christ eat at his table. That is why he invited Him. He loved the Lord for coming and giving him eternal life, but his love was nowhere as profound as the woman's. He felt that the weight of sin that had to be wiped away in order for him to sit at that table with the Christ was nothing compared to that of the woman.

In the parable, Christ indicated that her sins were ten times the amount of Simon's. Perhaps Jesus was simply reflecting Simon's estimation of his sin as compared to the woman's. Or maybe it was an accurate description. The woman accepted the magnitude of the debt she owed. When the Lord forgave it, she expressed her love for Him.

Both the woman and Simon are the debtors in the parable. Both are forgiven, and both are believers. Both will be in the kingdom. But the woman loved the Lord more deeply and served Him more fervently. Simon thought the Lord was thrilled to eat with him. The truth was that the Lord was more thrilled to be with her.

The Lord was teaching Simon, his child, through the woman. Hopefully, Simon learned the lesson: If he were going to be close to the King and earn His praise, he would need to have a clearer understanding of Christ's mercy to him and then extend that mercy to others.

The Gospel of Luke was written for believers. Simon and the sinful woman provide lessons for every believer. A major lesson is that every believer, regardless of past sins, can have intimate fellowship with the King and serve Him.

THE GOSPEL OF JOHN: EVANGELISTIC BOOK, OR SOMETHING ELSE?

JOHN CLAEYS

Tyler, Tx

I. INTRODUCTION

In the movie, *The Truman Show*, Truman is not aware that, since birth, he has been the star of the ultimate reality show. He does not realize that he lives in a large dome, covering several square miles, in which the show's producer controls the sun, wind, rain, and even ocean waves at the push of a button. A cast of thousands surrounds Truman, but he has no idea that every person in his world is simply an actor. For the show to continue, Truman must remain ignorant of the fact that he lives in an artificial world.

During his thirties, Truman becomes restless and suspicious. Finally beginning to understand his situation, he boards a sailboat in an attempt to leave his artificial world. The producer tries everything, including lying, to keep Truman from escaping this world. But Truman stands at the door to real life. A real, abundant life awaits him, but a competing voice with selfish motives urges him to stay in the artificial world.[1]

There is a sense in which unbelievers live in an artificial world, experiencing an artificial life—until they listen to the truth. But what is the truth? How does one escape the artificial life of an unbeliever and enter into God's abundant life? Where should we look for the answer to this question?

There are competing voices proclaiming that they have the answer. If you ask Christians how one can enter God's life, some say the answer is found in the Gospel of John. Others say that while John has some of the truth, other books of the Bible also show us the way to enter God's life. Can all these opinions be correct?

In order to decide which view we should believe, we will examine the Gospel of John carefully. Is John's Gospel *the* evangelistic book of the Bible, showing us *the* way to escape this artificial world, or does

---

[1] Adopted from Craig Brian Larson and Lori Quicke, *More Movie-Based Illustrations for Peaching and Teaching* (Grand Rapids, MI: Zondervan, 2004), 156-57.

it show *a* way or part of a way? Is John's Gospel unique among other books of the Bible, or is it simply one of many that include a saving message? We will discover that the answer to this question is critically important.

II. THE UNIQUENESS OF JOHN'S GOSPEL

A long-held view among theologians is that John's Gospel was written to supplement the Synoptics (Matthew, Mark, and Luke).[2] However, "there is nothing in the Fourth Gospel [John's Gospel] that gives any indication that the author intended to supplement the Synoptic Gospels and nothing that would give us any guide or assurance in using John in this way."[3] Ninety-two percent of John's Gospel is material unique to it.[4] This makes John's Gospel unique among the Gospels. Unique material indicates a unique purpose. As C. F. D. Moule stated:

> This Gospel [John's Gospel], unlike the others, answers the question, "What must I do to be saved?" The others [the Synoptics] mainly confine themselves to the story of discipleship; the Fourth Gospel speaks in terms…of belief and incorporation.[5]

III. THE PURPOSE STATEMENT OF JOHN'S GOSPEL: 10:10B OR 20:31?

Whether one sees John's Gospel as an evangelistic book or something else depends on what one sees as the purpose statement of the Gospel and how one views the role of the Upper Room Discourse (the Last Discourse) presented within the book.

Two verses—10:10b and 20:31—are typically cited as stating the Gospel's purpose. Those who understand 10:10b to be the purpose statement typically view the book as a hybrid of evangelistic teaching and discipleship teaching. On the other hand, many (but not all)

---

[2] Raymond E. Brown, *The Gospel According to John* (Garden City, NY: Doubleday & Company, 1966), xliv. *Synoptic* comes from two Greek words that, combined, literally mean "see together." Matthew, Mark, and Luke are called the *Synoptic Gospels* because they share so much in common.

[3] Ibid., xliv.

[4] Bruce Wilkinson and Kenneth Boa, *Talk Thru the Bible* (Nashville, TN: Thomas Nelson Publishers, 1983), 304.

[5] C. F. D. Moule, *The Birth of the New Testament* (London: Adam and Charles Black, 1962), 94.

of those who view 20:31 as the book's purpose statement generally understand John to be an evangelistic book.

Some, such as John A. T. Robinson and Raymond Brown, understand 20:31 to be the purpose statement, but suggest that John's purpose in writing his Gospel was to "root the believer deeper in his faith."[6] These (and others who side with their view) translate the verse in this way: "... that you may [continue to] have faith that Jesus is the Messiah." This understanding stems from viewing the Greek present tense as having a durative (continual) aspect. However, J. P. Louw effectively challenged the durative aspect of the present tense in 1975.[7] Louw concludes that the present tense is "aspectually neutral or unmarked, it is a zero tense. It may be used to denote present, past, or future time according to context..."[8] Thus, durative, or continual, aspect in Greek is not denoted by the present tense. Instead, the aspect of a verb in Greek is presented lexically (by means of context).

In conclusion, Louw warns: "...the aspectual value of a tense should not be pressed to the expense of the contextual structure of a passage."[9] In other words, the present tense should not be forced to make the verb show continuation if the context does not show it. Context, not tense, determines the aspect of a verb.

This is an important warning. The immediate context of John 20:31 shows that John's Gospel uses signs to prove that Jesus is the Christ so that his readers might believe in Him for eternal life.[10] Earlier in the Gospel, Jesus shows that one momentary act of believing is sufficient to receive eternal life.

This is illustrated, for example, in 3:14-15: "And as Moses lifted up the serpent in the wilderness, even so must the Son of Man be lifted up, that whoever believes in Him should not perish but have eternal life." Here, Jesus cites a scene recorded in Num 21:9: "So Moses made a bronze serpent, and put it on a pole; and so it was, if a serpent had bitten anyone when he looked at the bronze serpent, he lived." This was a simple declaration of a simple act. If anyone simply *looked at the*

---

[6] Brown, *John*, lxxviii. See, also, John A. T. Robinson, "The Destination and Purpose of St. John's Gospel," *New Testament Studies* 6 (1959-60): 117-31.

[7] J. P. Louw, "Verbal Aspect in the First Letter of John," *Neotestamentica*, 9 (1975): 98-104.

[8] Ibid., 102.

[9] Ibid., 104.

[10] Leon Morris aptly commented that using the present tense in 20:31 to show the importance of continual faith for believers "is reading a great deal into the tense and it is more probable that we should see an evangelistic aim whatever the tense" (*The Gospel According to John* [Grand Rapids, MI: Eerdmans, 1981], 856).

serpent, he lived. There is not a hint that one had to continue to look at that serpent till the day he died. (How ironic is that statement!) One look brought life from death. Jesus used this illustration to teach that, just as one look at the lifted serpent brought life, so one "look" of faith to Jesus for eternal life brings unending life to that individual.

In 4:13-14, Jesus again describes the reception of eternal life as being based on belief in a moment of time:

> Jesus answered and said to her, "Whoever drinks of this water will thirst again, but whoever drinks of the water that I shall give him will never thirst. But the water that I shall give him will become in him a fountain of water springing up into everlasting life."

The woman clearly understood something about the point Jesus was making. This is reflected in her reply: "Sir, give me this water, that I may not thirst, nor come here to draw" (4:15). She grasped the nature of saving faith even if she did not yet understand what He was offering to her. This woman understood that what He was offering was received once, with lasting results. She realized that she would not need to keep making return trips to draw this water. Once she accepted His offer at a point in time, she would possess it forever.

Clearly, John had already stipulated through Jesus' own illustrations, that saving faith needs to be exercised at only a moment in time, with everlasting results. Both the immediate context of 20:31 and the overall context of the book demonstrate that John did not intend his readers to interpret *believe* in 20:31 as a durative, or continual, faith.

Furthermore, the context of the book shows that John's Gospel is written with unbelievers in mind. This can be easily ascertained from verses such as: John 3:15-18, 36; 4:5-42 (especially v 42); 5:24; 6:35-40, 47; 7:35-37; 8:28-31, 56-58; 9:35-38; 10:1-30; 11:25-27; 12:10-11; 13:10-11; 14:6; 17:3-8, 20-21; 18:33-37; 19:30; 20:28-31; 21:25. Therefore, 20:31 demonstrates a purpose statement aimed at unbelievers.

In narrative literature, it is logical to place the purpose statement at either the beginning or end of the book. As Brown points out:

> Luke explains his purpose at the beginning of his Gospel (1:1-4), but John saves his statement of intention till the end. In selecting material to be included

> in the Gospel his goal has been to have people come to faith or increase in faith (disputed reading) in Jesus the Messiah, the Son of God, and through this faith to possess eternal life in his name.[11]

Luke places his purpose statement at the beginning of his narrative (Luke 1:1-4) because he is reporting to Theophilus, who likely financed Luke's research on the life, death, and resurrection of Jesus Christ. However, it seems that the apostle John places his purpose statement in 20:31, toward the end of his narrative account.[12]

Let us examine 20:30-31 to see why it qualifies as the overarching statement of John's Gospel:

> And truly Jesus did many other signs in the presence of His disciples, which are not written in this book; but these are written that you may believe that Jesus is the Christ, the Son of God, and that believing you may have life in His name.

Notice that John refers to the *signs* he has written *in this book*. These signs begin with Jesus' turning water into wine (2:1-11) and culminate in His death and resurrection (chaps. 19 and 20).[13] Because the final sign of John's Gospel occurs in chap. 20, John's statement in

---

[11] Raymond E. Brown, *An Introduction to the New Testament* (New York: Doubleday, 1997), 360. In citing Brown, Zane Hodges points out that the disputed reading has to do with whether the original reading had *believe* in a present tense or an aorist. The vast majority of manuscripts present *believe* in the aorist tense, while a small minority show it to be in present tense. Ultimately, as Hodges explains, this should not result in a difference in meaning (Zane Hodges, "Introducing John's Gospel: In the Upper Room with Jesus the Christ," *JOTGES* (Spring 2008): 30-31.

[12] Those who see 20:31 as the purpose statement of John's Gospel include: Edwin A. Blum, "John," *The Bible Knowledge Commentary: New Testament Edition*, eds. by John F. Walvoord and Roy B. Zuck (Wheaton, IL: Victor Books, 1983), 268, 344; Marcus Dods, "The Gospel of St. John," *The Expositor's Greek Testament* (Grand Rapids, MI: Eerdmans, 1980), 1:678-79; Morris, *John*, 39-40, 855-57; Moule, *The Birth of the New Testament*, 94; J. Dwight Pentecost, *The Words and Works of Jesus Christ* (Grand Rapids, MI: Zondervan, 1981), 506; Archibald Thomas Robertson, "The Fourth Gospel," *Word Pictures in the New Testament* (Nashville, TN: Broadman Press, 1932), 317; B. F. Westcott, *The Gospel According to St. John* (Grand Rapids, MI: Eerdmans, 1981), 297-98; Robert N. Wilkin, "The Gospel According to John," *The Grace New Testament Commentary* (Denton, TX: Grace Evangelical Society, 2010), 1:357.

[13] Note that when Jesus was asked what *sign* He could show the Jewish religious leaders in order to prove that He had the authority to do such things as cleanse the temple, He pointed to His death and resurrection (2:18-22). R. H. Lightfoot stated: "The crucifixion was to St. John doubtless the greatest sign of all" (*St. John's Gospel*, ed. C. F. Evans [Oxford, Clarendon, 1956], 336). On the other hand, Pentecost states: "The Resurrection in John's mind was the climactic sign authenticating the person and work of Christ" (*The Words and Works of Jesus Christ*, 506). However, based on Jesus' statement in 2:19, the crucifixion was only half of the ultimate sign; the resurrection was the necessary second half.

20:31 clearly reveals that he had written all the previous material in his Gospel to point his readers to believing in Jesus Christ for eternal life.

It should be noted here that John's Gospel may be the most Christological Gospel. George R. Beasley-Murray provides a long list of evidence for this.[14] The Christological factor in John is particularly represented by the title *Son of God*, which "is the outstanding feature of the revelation of God as Father in the Fourth Gospel."[15] This Christological feature is especially connected to soteriology.[16] This appears to be more evidence that the purpose statement of 20:31 is evangelistic.

There are some who believe that the purpose statement of John's Gospel is 10:10b: "… I have come that they may have life, and that they may have it more abundantly." However, Jesus' full statement in 10:10 is: "The thief does not come except to steal, and to kill, and to destroy. I have come that they may have life, and that they may have it more abundantly."

In John 10:10, Jesus states a contrast between death (*kill*)/ destruction (*steal, destroy*) and *life*. To further clarify this *life*, Jesus adds that it is life that is *abundant* (*perrison*). While *abundantly* is one meaning of *perrison,* its primary definition in John 10:10 seems to be "extraordinary, remarkable, of that which is not usually encountered among men."[17] In examining the usage of *perrison* in other NT passages, it seems that it can also carry the meaning of *beyond* (cf. Matt 5:37, 47; 11:9; Mark 7:36; Luke 12:4; 20:47; 1 Cor 12:23, 24; 15:10; 2 Cor 2:7; 10:8; Heb 6:17; 7:15) or *greater* (Matt 23:14; Mark 12:40).

Thus, the contrast is between that which the thief (representing any false teacher) offers versus that which Jesus offers. False teachers offer death and destruction while Jesus offers an extraordinary life, one that is remarkable in both its quantitative experience (unending; eternal life) and its qualitative experience (knowing God; John 17:3). It is more than the mere natural life that unbelievers possess.

To illustrate, years ago, I told an unbeliever that Jesus promises eternal life to anyone who simply believes Him for it. The recipient of my presentation stood up, remarked that everyone lives forever, and

---

[14] George R. Beasley-Murray, *John*, Word Biblical Commentary, 36 (Waco, TX: Word Books, 1987), lxxxi.

[15] Ibid., lxxxii.

[16] Ibid., lxxxiv, who cites Schnackenburg on this.

[17] BDAG, 651.

walked out of the room. To be fair, there is some truth to his statement. However, unbelievers do not experience the life Jesus offers, one that goes beyond the unbeliever's mere existence. He offers a remarkable life, a life that is both unending and the very life of God.

In other words, John 10:10 is not contrasting the experiences of different believers. In fact, there is not a hint of that in either the verse or the immediate context. The context of chap. 10 presents Jesus as the Christ (vv 14-18, 21, 24-30, 33-38). There is nothing in that chapter regarding Jesus offering some believers a more abundant life than other believers may experience. Instead, 10:10 is a contrast between what the thief offers and what Jesus offers to the world.

Furthermore, John 10:10 is a continuation of Jesus' instruction to the Pharisees following the sign of healing the blind man in chap. 9. Not only does 10:10 stem from the sign that Jesus did in chap. 9, but the verse is sandwiched between two signs: the healing of the blind man (chap. 9) and the resurrection of Lazarus (chap. 11). Between those two signs, no material is presented that could be called discipleship material. Thus, those who see 10:10b as the purpose statement of John's Gospel seem to ignore the immediate context, the signs of the Gospel, and John's purpose for the Gospel's signs.

It appears that the overriding reason many suggest 10:10b as the purpose statement of John has to do with their understanding of the Upper Room Discourse (the Last Discourse).[18] Because the Last Discourse *appears* to offer discipleship truth, many pivot to 10:10b to provide the purpose statement of John's Gospel.

IV. THE ROLE OF THE UPPER ROOM DISCOURSE IN JOHN'S GOSPEL

How one views the Last Discourse (chaps. 13–17) plays a determinative role in understanding the purpose of John's Gospel. If, for example, one sees the Last Discourse as material primarily for believers, then that individual will generally view John as a hybrid of

---

[18] In referring to the Upper Room Discourse, most are focusing on chaps. 13–17 of the Gospel of John. However, it is clear from 14:31b ("Arise, let us go from here") that chaps. 15–17 were presented after leaving the upper room. Thus, it is more accurate to refer to John 13–17 as the Last Discourse (Hodges, "Introducing John's Gospel," 32). (Though 18:1 states that after Jesus' spoken words to the Eleven, "He *went out* with His disciples over the Brook Kidron …," the words *went out* indicate that they went out of Jerusalem, not the upper room [Hodges, "Introducing John's Gospel," 32]).

evangelistic material and discipleship instruction. However, if one understands that the role of the Last Discourse is to demonstrate that Jesus is the Christ, that understanding typically lends itself to viewing the entire book as evangelistic.

As mentioned above, the purpose statement of the Gospel of John is found in 20:31, which presents John's Gospel as evangelistic. Since there is nothing in 20:31 that resembles discipleship material, we must ask: "How is the Last Discourse related to the purpose statement? How is the Last Discourse evangelistic?"

I have found thirty-nine pieces of evidence within the Last Discourse—enumerated below—indicating that the Gospel of John is evangelistic. Some specifically state an evangelistic focus, while many demonstrate that Jesus is the Christ, the Giver of eternal life.

1. The discourse is set within John's accounts of the eight signs around which his Gospel is arranged: Jesus turns water into wine (2:1-11); Jesus heals the nobleman's son (4:46-54); Jesus heals the paralytic (5:1-9); Jesus feeds the five thousand (6:1-13); Jesus walks on the water (6:16-21); Jesus raises Lazarus from the dead (11:1-45); and Jesus' death and resurrection (chaps. 19 and 20). The discourse is the prologue to the Gospel's eighth sign, which fulfills the Last Discourse's historical purpose: to prepare the disciples for Jesus' death, resurrection, and ascension into heaven.[19]

2. As the Christ, Jesus used this discourse to prepare His disciples for what was about to occur. He sought to prime them for His betrayal (13:18-19; 16:32), His death (15:20b-21; 16:20), His resurrection (16:20), and His ascension into heaven (13:33, 36; 14:1-2, 4; 16:16, 28; 17:4-5). In addition, He prepared them for the coming of the Holy Spirit (14:3, 16, 18-19; 16:7-11, 13-15; 17:11a, 13).[20]

3. No one ever faced death the way Jesus did. The way He faced death demonstrates that He is the Christ. For example, note 13:1:

---

[19] Hodges, "Introducing John's Gospel," 32.

[20] Though many view v 3 as referring to the Rapture, it seems more likely that this verse speaks of the promised coming of the Holy Spirit. (John 17:11a, 13 could be included in this same discussion.) Compare the last half of the verse ("I will come again and receive you to Myself; that where I am, there you may be also") with v 18 ("I will not leave you orphans; I will come to you"). Both make the promise of "I will come…" (Clearly, v 18 is connected to the promise of the Holy Spirit in vv 16-17. Jesus would not leave them as orphans because He would send the Holy Spirit to them.) A promise of the Rapture seems disjointed in this context—which speaks of His ascending to heaven in order to send the Holy Spirit to them—for nothing else is said about the future beyond Jesus preparing the disciples for His going away. How would the Rapture prepare them for His death, resurrection, and ascension into heaven?

"Now before the feast of the Passover, when Jesus knew that His hour had come that He should depart from this world to the Father, having loved His own who were in the world, He loved them to the end." He loved His followers to the very end of His life. In fact, the discourse closes with this prayer to the Father: "And I have declared to them Your name, and will declare it, that the love with which You loved Me may be in them, and I in them" (17:26). Instead of being anxious regarding what was about to transpire or seeking deliverance from His betrayal, suffering, and death, Jesus focused on His disciples, as He loved them to the end. During His last night with His disciples, He provided them with the perfect teaching to prepare them for His exit and the perfect example for them to follow (cf. 13:15).

4. Jesus showed that He is the Christ by demonstrating His perfect knowledge of what lay ahead and where He was going (13:10-11, 19, 21, 26-30, 38; 14:28-30; 16:2-4, 16, 32 [13:33; 14:19; 16:19]). Only the Christ—the One sent from the Father—could possess this foreknowledge.

5. Jesus demonstrated that He is the Christ by fulfilling Scripture (13:18). He fulfilled Scripture by choosing His apostles, including the one who would betray Him.

6. As the Christ, He gave His disciples the overarching commandment that they were to follow: They were to love as He had loved them (13:34-35; 15:12, 17). He provided them with the perfect example of how to love.

7. Jesus showed that He had the authority to send the Holy Spirit to indwell them (14:3, 16-18, 23; 15:26; 16:7-13, 16). Only the Christ has that kind of authority.

8. Jesus revealed that the Holy Spirit testifies of Him and glorifies Him (15:26; 16:14-15). For the third member of the Trinity to glorify Him demonstrates, above all, that Jesus is the Christ.

9. Jesus' words are the Father's words (14:10, 24; 15:15). Only the Christ, the Son of God, could give this pronouncement, particularly the words of 15:15: "…all things that I heard from My Father I have made known to you."[21]

10. Jesus revealed that He is in the Father, and the Father is in Him (14:10-11). The Jews saw this as blasphemous and is one reason they sought to kill Him. After all, Jesus "said that God was His Father,

[21] Even a prophet would not make this claim of directly hearing from the Father, as it was the Holy Spirit who gave prophets their messages.

making Himself equal with God" (John 5:18), and He stated: "I and My Father are one" (10:30). He repeats this statement in 17:21, when He declares that He and the Father are one. Furthermore, Jesus announced that the one who hates Him hates the Father (15:23), which is another declaration that He and the Father are one, indicating that He is the Christ.

11. Jesus declared that the one who believes in Him will do greater works (14:12). For Him to be able to promise that by believing in Him, greater works would ensue, indicates an authority that only the Christ could guarantee.

12. Jesus also claimed to have such great authority that if His apostles ask anything in His name, He will do it (14:13-14) and the Father will do it (15:16; 16:23-24). Only the Christ has such authority granted by the Father.

13. Jesus declared that the one who keeps His word will be loved by the Father, and that, as a result, He and the Father will abide in him (14:23). This is a bold declaration that He could make only if He were the Christ.

14. Jesus proclaimed that the one who loves Him will be loved by the Father (14:21). If He were a mere man, this would be the height of arrogance, on the level of megalomania. Only the Christ could make this statement in truth.

15. Jesus claimed to give peace to His disciples that the world cannot provide (14:27; 16:33). Only the One sent from God could declare this kind of authority with veracity.

16. Jesus declared that those who abide in Him will bear much spiritual fruit, and that those who do not abide in Him cannot bear spiritual fruit (15:1-8). No mere man could make this claim.

17. Jesus proclaimed that by keeping His words, His disciples will have full joy (15:11). Again, this would be delusional if declared by a mere man.

18. Jesus declared that because His disciples belong to Him, they are not of this world (15:19). Again, only One sent from heaven could truthfully make this claim.

19. Jesus revealed that because He came into the world, revealing the Father, the world has no excuse to keep it from being judged (15:22-24). To claim that He can keep people from judgment must mean that He is the Christ.

20. Jesus revealed that His teaching will keep His disciples from spiritually stumbling (16:1). Not even the great teachers of the past could make this claim. But the Christ can make this declaration in truth.

21. Jesus declared that everything the Father has belongs to Him (16:15). If He were not the Christ, this would be the statement of a madman.

22. Jesus revealed that He came from the Father (16:27-28; 17:21). Only the Christ could make this statement in truth.

23. Jesus demonstrated an understanding of something that only God could know for sure. He showed that He knew those who had believed in Him for eternal life (eleven of the apostles), as opposed to Judas, when He stated: "…you are clean, but not all of you" (13:10). After all, "The Lord knows those who are His" (2 Tim 2:19).

24. In keeping with the evangelistic nature of John's Gospel, Jesus proclaimed in 14:6: "I am the way, the truth, and the life. No one comes to the Father except through Me." This proclamation clearly presents Jesus as the Christ.

25. Jesus revealed that He would prepare a place for believers to be with Him in eternity (14:2-3). His ability to do that must mean that He is the Christ, the Giver of eternal life.

26. Jesus revealed that the one who has seen Him has seen the Father (14:9). He is the perfect Representative of the Father. That is because He is the Christ sent from the Father.

27. Jesus disclosed to the Eleven that, "You are already clean because of the word which I have spoken to you" (15:3), thereby reminding readers of the Gospel that the Eleven had eternal life because they had believed Jesus' promise.

28. Jesus declared Himself to be the vine and believers to be the branches. Furthermore, He revealed that if believers abide (remain) in Him, they will bear fruit (15:1-5). In addition, Jesus revealed to those who believe in Him that apart from Him, they can do nothing (15:5). To declare such life-giving ability to those who believe in Him indicates that He is the Christ.

29. Jesus revealed to His disciples that He would send the Holy Spirit. He then revealed the Holy Spirit's role in evangelism:

> "And when He has come, He will convict the world of sin, and of righteousness, and of judgment: of sin,

> because they do not believe in Me; of righteousness, because I go to My Father and you see Me no more; of judgment, because the ruler of this world is judged" (16:8-11).

This truth fits perfectly into the evangelistic Gospel of John.

30. Jesus announced that He is the Giver of eternal life (17:2). This is the definition of *the Christ.*

31. In 17:3, Jesus revealed that eternal life is knowing God. Thus, when one believes Jesus' promise of eternal life, that person has the very life of God. The recipient of Jesus' promise knows God in a way that no unbeliever does.

32. Jesus revealed that He had finished the work the Father sent Him to do (17:4), which was to prepare individuals to receive eternal life. This declared Him to be the Christ.

33. Jesus revealed that He shared glory with the Father before the world was created (17:5, 22). Only the Christ could make that statement.

34. Jesus declared that the Father sent Him into the world (17:18, 21). That He came from the Father into the world demonstrates that He is the Christ.

35. Jesus, once again, distinguished between those who had received eternal life (the eleven) and the one who did not receive it, Judas (17:12), making a clear distinction between those who have received life and those who have not. In doing so, Jesus showed that those who believe His promise are no longer part of the fallen world, just as He is not part of the world (17:14, 16).

36. Jesus prayed that His followers would have His joy fulfilled in them (17:13). To have His joy fulfilled in them indicates a supernatural source, which would be the Christ.

37. Jesus prayed for those who will believe in Him in the future (17:20). The inclusion of this statement indicates the evangelistic thrust of John's Gospel.

38. The Father loved Him before the world began (17:24). This means that He is the preexistent One, the Christ.

39. Jesus declared that, while the world does not know God, those who have believed Jesus' promise of eternal life do know God (17:25). That Jesus has the authority to deliver those who believe in Him from the world demonstrates that He is the Christ.

Therefore, chaps. 13–17, as well as chaps. 18–19, are included in John's gospel to demonstrate that Jesus is the Christ. These chapters declare again and again that Jesus is, indeed, the Christ. In fact, chaps. 13–17 are preparatory to chaps. 18–19, which present the eighth—and greatest—of the signs in the Gospel of John (cf. 2:18-22). Of course, those signs are presented to lead people to believe in Jesus as the Christ, the Giver of eternal life.

After presenting the eight signs, chosen by the apostle John and the Holy Spirit to demonstrate that Jesus is the Christ, John explains why he included those signs:

> And truly Jesus did many other signs in the presence of His disciples, which are not written in this book; but these are written that you may believe that Jesus is the Christ, the Son of God, and that believing you may have life in His name (John 20:30-31).

V. THE ROLE OF JESUS' DEATH AND RESURRECTION IN JOHN'S GOSPEL

The purpose statement of John's Gospel, 20:31, states that one receives eternal life by believing that Jesus is the Christ, that is, the Giver of eternal life.[22] There is nothing in the purpose statement regarding believing in Jesus' death and resurrection. In fact, there is nothing in the entire Gospel of John about believing in Jesus' death and resurrection to gain eternal life.

We need to recognize that, as the Christ, it was necessary for Jesus to die on the cross to atone for sin (to satisfy God's demand regarding sin) and to rise from the dead in victory over sin and death. His death

---

[22] That *the Christ* in John's Gospel refers to Jesus as the Giver of eternal life can be seen in at least four ways. First, *the Christ* appears in the evangelistic encounter with the Samaritan woman in John 4. The Samaritans who believed Jesus for eternal life remarked about Him: "… this is indeed *the Christ*, the Savior of the world" (4:42). In that episode, Jesus identified Himself to the woman as the Giver of eternal life (cf. 4:10, 13-14). This means that *the Christ* is the Savior who gives eternal life. Second, Peter identifies Jesus as *the Christ*, the Giver of eternal life (6:68-69). Third, the term *the Christ* appears twenty-one times in John's Gospel—more times than in any other book of the Bible—the book that repeatedly shows that Jesus gives eternal life to the one who believes Him for it. Fourth, when presented with Jesus' ability to give eternal life to whoever believes Him for it, Martha immediately identifies Him as *the Christ* (11:25-27).

and resurrection were accomplished so that individuals may receive the life of God.[23]

However, Jesus' death and resurrection were one of the eight signs in John's Gospel. Note that when the Jews asked Jesus for a sign that would demonstrate His authority, He replied: "Destroy this temple, and in three days I will raise it up" (2:19). While the Jews thought that He was speaking of the temple in Jerusalem (2:20), John explains:

> But He was speaking of the temple of His body. Therefore, when He had risen from the dead, His disciples remembered that He had said this to them; and they believed the Scripture and the word which Jesus had said (John 2:21-22).

Therefore, Jesus proclaimed that the ultimate sign demonstrating His authority is His death ("Destroy this temple" [His body]) and resurrection ("I will raise it up"). Combined, His death and resurrection comprise the final sign in John's Gospel.[24]

The apostle John presents these signs in his Gospel so that one might receive eternal life by believing Jesus' promise of it. Believing the signs does not produce life. However, by believing the signs, one can recognize that Jesus is the Giver of eternal life. It is by believing Jesus' promise of eternal life that one receives God's life, not by believing one or more of the signs in the Gospel of John.

VI. CONCLUSION

In this article, we have identified the uniqueness of John's Gospel and have found that nearly all of it (92%) presents material not included in the Synoptic Gospels. Unique material indicates a unique purpose.

We then explored the purpose statement of John's Gospel to determine whether 10:10b or 20:31 is the book's purpose statement. In doing so, we have concluded that 20:31 is the purpose statement of John.

---

[23] Many other aspects of Jesus' life were necessary for making it possible for individuals to receive life in His name. Some examples are: His deity, His virgin birth, His fulfillment of more than 300 OT prophecies, His sinless life, etc. But God does not require one to believe these in order to receive life in His name.

[24] Jesus uses the singular *sign* for both His death and resurrection, showing that the two events combine to make up one sign.

We examined the Last Discourse to determine its role in fulfilling John's stated purpose. We concluded that its role is to demonstrate that Jesus is the Christ, which fits the evangelistic purpose of John's Gospel.

Finally, we looked at the role of Jesus' death and resurrection in John's Gospel in order to understand how it fits the purpose statement of John. We have concluded that Jesus' death and resurrection combine to be the final sign in the Gospel of John, pointing to Jesus as the Christ. In drawing this conclusion, we have come to understand that while Jesus' death and resurrection were critically important to providing eternal life, these two events are not part of the salvific message of John. Instead, they are signs pointing to Jesus as the Christ. The salvific message of John is: Jesus grants eternal life to anyone who believes His promise of eternal life.

Our conclusion is that John's Gospel is evangelistic. It is the one book of the Bible written to unbelievers for the purpose of showing them how to receive eternal life (life with God forever). As the Gospel of John presents repeatedly, Jesus' promise is that He gives eternal life to anyone who simply believes Him for it.

PREPARING TO HAVE A LAVISH KINGDOM ENTRANCE (PART 2)[1]

DAVID JANSSEN

Pastor of Spiritual Growth
Grace Community Bible Church
Sandy, Utah

IV. THE RESULTS OF GROWING SPIRITUALLY, OR NOT (2 PET 1:8-9)

Verse 8 spells out the positive benefits for the believer who possesses and develops the seven virtues enumerated in vv 5-7. Verse 9 outlines the negative consequences for the believer who lacks these virtues.

A. The Positive Results of Possessing and Increasing in These Seven Virtues (1:8)

Verse 8a says, "For if these qualities are yours and are increasing, they…". Peter's use of *for if* to begin the verse makes this a conditional statement. To qualify, a believer must meet two conditions: 1) he must *have* these seven virtues, and 2) they must *be increasing*. Although *having* these virtues is unmeasurable, the concept is that they should be observable to others.[2]

However, it is not enough to merely *have* these virtues in our lives to some degree; we are to grow in these areas as well. The Greek word for *increasing* is *pleonazo*. It is used nine times in the NT, including eight times by Paul and this one time by Peter. The Greek form of this word "always expresses the notion of development, denoting a process of growing, multiplying, or increasing."[3] God desires and expects the growth of these seven virtues, and we should be taking intentional and

---

[1] Editor's Note: This is the conclusion of Janssen's article on 2 Pet 1:1-11. Part 1 was published in the Spring 2025 edition of the *JOTGES*. Both parts comprise the paper he wrote for the GES National Conference in 2024. The topic of the conference was *The Epistles of Peter*. The audio of his presentation can be found at www.faithalone.org.

[2] "Since special emphasis is placed on *acts that demonstrate the character*, the term ["virtue"] should not be understood as simply a recognition of the internal character of the heart." Green, *Jude & 2 Peter*, 92. (Emphasis added.)

[3] NIDNTTE, vol. 3, 778.

specific steps to improve on each of them. Ask yourself, for example, "*How am I doing on godliness?*" and "*What am I doing today to practice increased self-control?*" Local church leaders should encourage believers to cultivate each of these virtues and provide concrete guidance on how to do so.

If a believer has these virtues and they are increasing, the outcome will be that "they do not make you useless nor unproductive" (v 8). The Greek word for *useless* is found eight times in the NT. It is also translated as "careless," "idle," and "lazy."[4] James uses *useless* in Jas 2:20.[5] There is nothing positive about being useless!

The Greek word translated as "*productive*" means "fruit," so if something is *unproductive*, the result is that it is *unfruitful*, which is how the word is translated in the NASB95 and NKJV. A fruit tree is expected to bear fruit, but when it does not, it is not accomplishing the purpose for which it was created.

Peter uses a double negative, "not…useless…nor unproductive," rather than approaching this with the positive words *fruitful* and *productive*. Does he do this for the purpose of motivation? When I discuss living an eternally productive life with believers, they often hesitate to make that commitment, even if they believe that God will reward such a life. On the other hand, when asked if they want to *waste* their life, they consistently want to avoid that. Peter's double negative would generate a stronger response. No believer wants his life to be useless and unfruitful.

Peter explains that a person with these *increasing* virtues will be useful and productive as they serve Jesus, thereby resulting "in the true knowledge of our Lord Jesus Christ" (v 8c). This is the third time in this passage (vv 1-11) that the phrase *true knowledge*, from the Greek *epignosis* occurs. All four of the occurrences of *in* or *through* with *epignosis* ("knowledge") in 2 Peter (1:2, 3, 8; 2:20) are followed by *God*, *Him*, and/or *Jesus* or *Christ*. So, the concept of *leading to*[6] a deeper personal relationship with Jesus fits well with all four occurrences.

---

[4] The NASB20 translates this adjective, *argos*, as follows: *careless* (one time), *idle* (four), *lazy* (one), *useless* (two).

[5] The Majority Text has the Greek word for *dead* instead of *useless*. The three uses of *dead* in James 2 mean *useless*.

[6] Colossians 2:2 is a passage that contains the same Greek phrase, *in (eis)* and *true knowledge (epignosis)*. Murray Harris uses Col 2:2 to illustrate the various ways that *in* can be understood. In Col 2:2 it can mean at least the following things: 1) *towards* true knowledge (direction); 2) *in the sphere* (locative); 3) *for* (end goal); 4) *leading to* (consecutive); or 5) *until it reaches fullness*

Peter's point is that as believers grow spiritually by increasing in these virtues, they will be useful and productive as they serve Jesus, leading to relational closeness to Him. How does being useful and productive in serving Jesus lead to this relational closeness?

My marriage is a great example. I was single until, at the age of 25, I married my wife, Anne. At that time, I had an entrenched habit of not making my bed in the morning. My reasoning was relatively straightforward: No one was going to see my messy bed during the day, and I was just going to get back into it again that night. When I got married, Anne seemed to think the bed should be made every day!

Now, my logic was still true—no one was going to see the messy bed, and we were going to get back into that bed that evening. What to do? I love my wife and want to have a good and close relationship with her. So, even though I didn't see the point, I began making the bed every morning. Forty-two years later, I am still making the bed (OK… she makes it sometimes). You see, I am not a useless or unproductive husband. And pleasing her did indeed lead to a closer relationship with her. My actions led to knowing her better.

When we develop these seven virtues, we are useful and productive. When we serve Jesus, it draws us closer to Him. This is how *serving and doing ministry* will directly improve our relationship with Jesus!

B. The Negative Results of *Not* Having These Seven Virtues (1:9)

Verse 9 says, "For the one who lacks these [qualities] is blind [or] short-sighted, having forgotten [his] purification from his former sins." Peter uses three adjectives to describe a person who does not have these virtues. He says that the person is: 1) blind, 2) short-sighted, and 3) forgetful. The meaning of *blind* is fairly straightforward: the person can't see! Believers can be blind to the spiritual aspect of life, rarely thinking about it. Spiritual matters are just not on this believer's radar.

A believer can be short-sighted and focus on only the things immediately in front of them in the physical world. Once again, spiritual concerns are barely in view. By being short-sighted, a believer is not focusing on the return of Christ (2 Peter 3) because that is too far away and lies beyond their area of concern. For this believer, there is no connection between eternity and how he should live today. The

(temporal). The consecutive use—*leading to* best fits 2 Pet 1.8. Murray Harris, *Prepositions and Theology in the Greek New Testament* (Grand Rapids, MI: Zondervan, 2012), 102.

person simply does not see the importance of spiritual activities such as praying, reading the Bible, or even attending church regularly; none of these things is a priority. Jesus speaks of this sort of believer in Mark 4:18-19: "And others are the ones sown [with seed] among the thorns; these are the ones who have heard the word, but the worries of the world, and the deceitfulness of wealth, and the desires for other things enter and choke the word, and it becomes unfruitful." The believer who is focused on worries, wealth, and desires for other things is blind and short-sighted.

The third characteristic of a believer who lacks these seven virtues is forgetfulness. Verse 9 says, "having forgotten [his] purification from his former sins." What *former sins* is Peter talking about? Is Peter going back to the time when the person believed in Jesus for eternal life and experienced purification or forgiveness? Or is he talking about sins that the person committed earlier in his Christian life that he had confessed and been forgiven of? In either case, he has forgotten.

When believers drift away from their walk with the Lord and therefore lack these virtues, they have forgotten about Jesus' forgiveness.

C. Summary of Verses 8 and 9

Believers who have eternal life may or may not obey God and cultivate these seven virtues (v 8). If believers *do* work on developing these godly characteristics, their service for Jesus will be effective, and they will walk more closely with Him. If believers fail to cultivate these virtues in their lives, they will be clueless about spiritual matters and will not walk closely with Jesus. These believers are spiritually worthless in their service to Christ.

V. THE SECOND COMMAND: KNOW THAT YOU ARE CALLED TO GROW AND CHOSEN TO SERVE (1:10)

A. Conclusion with a Command (1:10)

Second Peter 1:10 says, "Therefore, brothers [and sisters], be all the more diligent to make certain about His calling and choice of you; for as long as you practice these things, you will never stumble…"

Peter's *therefore* introduces the command that believers *be... diligent*. This is the second command in this letter; *supply* was the first (1:5). Commands are important because they are the clearest way in which God can say: "This is what I value, what is important, and what is best for your life."

Peter *commands* believers to be diligent (see also 3:14). The word *diligent* means "to work hard, to do one's best."[7] God is commanding believers to expend energy "to make certain" about "His calling and choice of you." But what does Peter mean by "calling and choice of you"?

B. How "Calling and Choice of You" Is Commonly Understood: A Reformed Perspective (1:10)

The most common interpretation stems from a Reformed or Calvinistic perspective, which posits that *calling and choosing* refer to a pre-temporal decision by God to *call and choose* specific individuals for eternal life. The five points of Calvinism are summarized in the acronym TULIP, and the *U* represents "Unconditional Election."[8] In *The Five Points of Calvinism,* the authors proclaim:

> The doctrine of election declares that God, before the foundation of the world, chose certain individuals from among the fallen members of Adam's race to be the objects of His undeserved favor. These, and these only, He purposed to save.[9]

In this view, election or choosing is about God's determining who will be saved.

In his commentary on 2 Peter and Jude, John MacArthur wrote, "*Calling* and *choosing* are inseparable realities indicating God's effectual call of believers to salvation based on His sovereign election of them in eternity past."[10]

According to this viewpoint, the only way a person can be certain about their election to eternal life is to focus on how they are living

---

[7] Louw & Nida, 68.63 s.v., *spoudazo*. Accessed in Accordance.

[8] The Greek word for *choice* here in 1:10 is related to the word translated "elect" eight times in NASB20.

[9] David Steele, Curtis Thomas, S. Lance Quinn, *The Five Points of Calvinism: Defined, Defended, and Documented* (Phillipsburg, NJ: P&R Publishing, 1963, 2004), 27.

[10] John MacArthur, *The MacArthur New Testament Commentary: 2 Peter & Jude* (Chicago, IL: Moody Publishers, 2005), 44. The italicized words are bolded in the original.

for God right now. MacArthur is clear: "The only legitimate basis for assurance has nothing to do with a past event when one 'made a decision,' but is based on the reality of present trust in Christ's atoning work, *as evidenced by one's present pattern of faith, obedience, righteousness, and love for the Lord*."[11] In other words, from this perspective, a person's good works are the evidence of whether or not the person is saved.

C. "Calling and Choice of You" from a Free Grace Perspective (1:10)

From a Free Grace perspective, 2 Pet 1:1-11 is all about spiritual growth and service. The phrase "His calling and choice of you" has nothing to do with a supposed decision by God in eternity past to select who will and will not be given eternal life.[12] The possession of eternal life is determined by whether or not someone believes in Jesus for eternal life (1 Tim 1:16). When a person believes, they *have* eternal life (John 6:47), which can never be lost. Assurance of salvation is found in the promises of God (e.g., 1 John 5.11-13), not in our performance (i.e., good works).

To "be all the more diligent to make certain about His calling and choice of you" is about certainty regarding our spiritual growth and effectiveness (*useful* and *productive* [1:8]).

Several Free Grace authors have commented on "His calling and choice of you":

- Ken Yates presents two views: "One possible answer is that He has called believers to good works.... If God has called believers to good works, then they should be consistent in doing what God has called them to do.... Another option is...while the believer knows he or she has eternal life by faith alone in Christ, others 'see' that life in our actions."[13]
- Bob Wilkin says, "2 Peter 1:10 refers to being called and chosen *to have a rich entrance into the kingdom* (2 Pet. 1:11)."[14]
- Zane Hodges says, "all Christians have been given a 'royal' summons by God Himself, 'who calls [us] into His own

[11] Ibid., 35.

[12] Bob Wilkin blog at www.faithalone.org, *Does God Elect People to Salvation?* (Sept. 20, 2024).

[13] Ken Yates's blog at www.faithalone.org, *Abundantly Entering the Kingdom* (2 Peter 1:10-11) (Jan. 1, 2015).

[14] Bob Wilkin blog at www.faithalone.org, *Does God Elect People to Salvation?* (Sept. 20, 2024).

> kingdom and glory' (1 Thes. 2:12). And a supremely significant part of that glory is the privilege of co-reigning with Christ (2 Tim. 2:12; Rev. 2:27-27, 3:21). But not all Christians are *chosen* to co-reign."[15]

Although expressed slightly differently, these ideas all point in the same direction—toward Christian living—and have nothing to do with proving one's salvation. As I see it, believers are *called to grow* and *chosen to serve* in this life, resulting in both present life benefits and eternal rewards.

A consolidation of the ideas expressed by various Free Grace authors might be stated in this way: When believers are growing spiritually and serving Jesus (right now), they do good works (now) and others see them demonstrating their new life (now), leading to the reward of a rich *entrance* into the kingdom (future) and potentially co-reigning with Jesus (future).

Suffice it to say, we are not *required* to grow and *forced* to serve; rather, God respects our free choice, and He *calls* us to grow and *chooses* us to serve. Each is a great privilege and opportunity for us as believers! What we do with this calling and choosing is left up to us, but God is clear in His command to be diligent and to embrace this royal summons in your life.

God's "calling us to grow" is spelled out in 2 Pet 1:5-7, where God commands believers to *add* to their faith. His "choice of you" to serve is reflected in v 8, which indicates that believers can be useful and productive in serving Jesus as they grow spiritually.

At the end of v 10, Peter says, "for as long as you practice these things, you will never stumble." The phrase *these things* points back to the two commands Peter has given: *supply* in v 5 and *be all the more diligent* in v 10. Believers who obey (*practice*) these commands will not stumble in their spiritual lives. The word *never* indicates that when a Christian *is* practicing these two commands, he is not stumbling.

D. Called to Grow and Chosen to Serve, as Supported by the Context

The phrase "His calling and choice of you" must be understood in the context of not just these 11 verses (2 Pet 1:1-11), but the entire book of 2 Peter.

---

[15] Hodges, *2 Peter*, 30-31.

Returning to the word *call* used in v 3, Peter uses it in v 10 with the same meaning—"a summons to believers to grow spiritually"—adding the phrase *choice of you*.

Here are eleven reasons, based on the context, supporting the conclusion that believers are *called to grow* and *chosen to serve*:

1. This letter was written to believers who have eternal life (i.e., they have faith) and whose salvation is not doubted or questioned by Peter. Therefore, Peter's purpose here is to encourage them in their *spiritual growth*.
2. At three points in the passage (vv 2, 3, 8), Peter talks about these Christians' knowing Jesus in a more intimate and experiential way (*true knowledge*). He is not writing to believers about how to have assurance of eternal life, but about how to grow closer to Jesus in their spiritual walk. This is about *spiritual growth*.
3. Verses 2-4 focus on God's granting us everything we need to *live* a godly life, not on receiving or being assured of eternal life. This is about *spiritual growth*.
4. The first command, "*supply*" (v 5), is something believers do in addition to the faith they already have. This is about *spiritual growth*.
5. What is to be supplied *by* the believer are seven virtues, and they are to be increasing (i.e., growing; vv 5-7). This is about *spiritual growth*.
6. If the list of virtues in vv 5-7 were to be an indicator of possessing eternal life, what would be the passing grade? How would these virtues be evaluated? Most believers' spiritual lives are a mixture of these virtues to various degrees, so when could a person have assurance of salvation based on this list? Verses 5-7 are about a believer's *spiritual growth*, not a test to determine election.
7. Verse 8 does NOT say, "For if these [qualities] are yours and are increasing, *then you will know you have eternal life!*" Instead, it says, "For if these [qualities] are yours and are increasing, *they do not make you useless nor*

unproductive..." This is about being useful and productive *in serving Jesus.*

8. Verse 9 does NOT say, "For the one who lacks these [qualities] is *not saved*." Instead, it says, "For the one who lacks these [qualities] is blind or short-sighted, having forgotten his purification from his former sins." This is about the lack of *spiritual growth*.
9. Verse 10 does NOT say, "to make certain about His calling and choice of you *so you will know you are saved!*" But it does say, "for as long as you practice these things, you will never stumble..." The second half of the verse, immediately after "His calling and choice of you," is about *spiritual growth*!
10. The word *choice* in the phrase, "His calling and choice of you," is often taken to mean God's choosing people in eternity past to be saved. However, in Shawn Lazar's excellent book, *Chosen to Serve: Why Divine Election Is to Service, Not to Eternal Life,* he concludes, "There isn't a single verse in the entire Bible that speaks about God's electing individuals to eternal life."[16] He comments on 2 Pet 1:10-11, "Those rewards will be given to believers who fulfill the calling to holiness and fulfill their vocational election to do good works (Eph 2:10)."[17]
11. In the last verse of this letter (3:18), Peter commands: "But grow in the grace and knowledge of our Lord and Savior Jesus Christ..." He begins his letter (1:1-11) by talking about *spiritual growth* and ends his letter by commanding it.

---

[16] Shawn Lazar, *Chosen to Serve: Why Divine Election Is to Service, not to Eternal Life* (Denton, TX: Grace Evangelical Society, 2017), 14.

[17] Ibid., 240.

VI. THE FUTURE RESULT OF GROWING AND SERVING JESUS (1:11)

A. The Future Result of Believers' Obeying God's Two Commands (1:5, 10) Is a Lavish Entrance into the Eternal Kingdom (1:11)

Peter describes a *specific* type of entrance into the kingdom, one that "will be abundantly supplied to you" (v 11). The Greek word for "abundantly" is an adverb, and it modifies the verb *supplied.* It is found four times in the NT.[18] The three uses outside of 2 Peter are translated as "richly."

For believers who supply, or *add,* seven virtues to their faith, God is going to *richly* supply or *add* (same word as in v 5) to their entrance into the kingdom! According to Bauchkham, "The verb here ["supplied"] indicates the lavish provision made by the divine generosity."[19] This is a reward for believers who grow spiritually and serve Jesus!

B. What Is the Eternal Kingdom? (1:11)

Verse 11 is the only place in the Bible where the phrase *eternal kingdom* is found. Ultimately, we are promised "new heavens and a new earth" (2 Pet 3:13), but the eternal kingdom begins with Jesus' 1,000-year reign on earth. Former Dallas Theological Seminary professor Stanley Toussaint compares the 1,000-year kingdom to a front porch, where people gather and visit for a while before entering the house.[20] The house in Toussaint's analogy represents the new heavens and the new earth. The house and the porch together represent the eternal kingdom of God. Believers will be participants in both the 1,000-year kingdom and the new heavens and new earth.

C. When Does This "Abundant Entrance" Take Place? (1:11)

Rewards are given out to believers at the Judgment Seat (*bema*) of Christ (2 Cor 5:10). Theologian and author John Claeys argues persuasively that the Judgment Seat of Christ will take place after the

---

[18] Colossians 3:16 "richly dwells," 1 Tim 6:17 "richly supplies," Titus 3:6 "richly poured out," and 2 Pet 1:11 "abundantly supplied."

[19] Bauchkham, *2 Peter*, 191.

[20] Stanley Toussaint, speaking at the Grace Evangelical Society National Conference, 2012.

Tribulation.[21] He proposes that Christ's rule begins 75 days after His physical arrival on planet Earth.[22] The beginning of Christ's 1,000-year reign seems the most logical place for "the entrance into the eternal kingdom of our Lord and Savior Jesus Christ" (2 Pet 1:11). The beginning of Christ's 1,000-year reign will undoubtedly be a majestic event beyond anything humanity has ever seen or could even imagine!

The ultimate endgame for believers is being with Jesus in His kingdom—both here on earth for 1,000 years and then in the new heavens and new earth for eternity. Second Peter tells believers how to live so that their entrance into that kingdom is rich, abundant, and grand!

VII. CONCLUSION

Many believers miss out on what God wants to do in and through them. They stop at just knowing they will spend eternity with Jesus, unaware of God's royal summons to discipleship, spiritual growth, and service. Peter rectifies that gap in our thinking.

As believers, God has given us everything we need to *live a godly life* that pleases Jesus. When we act on what God has provided, specifically His promises, we are able to share in His divine character and display to others what Jesus is like. Peter first commands believers to *develop* seven virtues and continue to *increase* them (i.e., grow in them). This results in fruitful and productive believers as they *serve* Jesus. Spiritual growth, at its heart, is experientially knowing Jesus more every day.

Peter's second command, which is foundational to a believer's perspective on his life, is to have solid conviction (v 10) about the fact that we have been *called to grow* and *chosen to serve*. To borrow a phrase from *The Blues Brothers*: "We're on a mission from God."[23] This attitude should motivate us to take spiritual growth seriously and serve Jesus intentionally.

Growing spiritually and serving Jesus has many benefits, not only in this life, but also in the life to come. In 2 Pet 1:1-10, Peter exhorts and encourages believers to grow spiritually and serve Jesus. In v 11,

---

[21] John Claeys, "When is the Judgment Seat of Christ?," *Journal of the Grace Evangelical Society*, Spring 2018: 35-45.

[22] Merrill F. Unger, *Unger's Bible Dictionary*, "Judgment Seat of Christ," (Chicago, IL: Moody Press, 1980), 622.

[23] 1980 Universal Pictures movie, *The Blues Brothers*, starring John Belushi and Dan Aykroyd. The sentence, "We're on a mission from God," is repeated with much conviction a number of times throughout the movie!

he defines our reward for doing so: a lavish, rich, *abundantly supplied* entrance into the kingdom!

Isn't that the kind of entrance you want?

DID THEY REALLY BELIEVE? (JOHN 2:23)[1]

BY HERSHALL SPRADLEY

I. A COMPARISON OF KEY THEOLOGICAL IDEAS IN THE GOSPELS OF LUKE AND JOHN[2]

There are key theological differences between the Gospels of Luke and John. These differences arise, in part, because the books have different purposes and are intended for different audiences. It is rare for an author of Scripture to explicitly state the reason for his work. But John gives the purpose of his Gospel in John 20:30-31:

> Many other signs Jesus also did in the sight of His disciples which are not written in this book. But these have been written in order that you would believe that Jesus is the Christ, the Son of God, and that believing you would have life in His name. (author's translation)

Luke states his purpose in Luke 1:1-4:

> Since many have undertaken to write a narrative concerning the things that have been fulfilled among us, just as they who became the eyewitnesses from the beginning and ministers of the word handed them down to us, it seemed good also to me, having followed closely all things from the beginning accurately, to write to you in order, most excellent Theophilus, in order that you could know the full truth concerning the words that you were taught. (author's translation)

From these purpose statements, we can make some observations. John's audience is unbelievers. He writes to people who are outside the church. This is the only book in the Bible addressed to unbelievers.

---

[1] Editor's Note: This article comes from a longer paper by Spradley entitled "Excursus on Luke's Gospel." The material before the discussion on John 2:23 is a summary of the first part of the original paper.

[2] Editor's Note: Spradley chose Luke because it is the only Synoptic Gospel that directly states its purpose.

Luke is addressed to insiders. He writes to those who have believed in Christ for eternal life and are a part of the church. The *us* in Luke's purpose statement refers to the believing community. Theophilus is a believer. He has been instructed in Christian truth. Luke wants him to know the certainty of this truth—that it is firmly rooted in history.[3] We could generalize the audience as being the broader believing community.

When we consider the purpose and audience of the two books, we can draw some conclusions. John writes to unbelievers, emphasizing the gift of eternal life offered by Jesus Christ to those who believe in Him.[4] Luke writes to believers, highlighting what it means to follow Jesus as His disciple. John and Luke clearly teach the distinction between what we often refer to as *salvation* and *discipleship.*

One of the most significant failures of the present-day Church has been its failure to distinguish between salvation and discipleship, resulting in a confused evangelistic message. John's message of eternal life and Luke's message of discipleship are two distinct messages that invite two different responses from two different audiences. Those who respond to John's message know Jesus as Savior. Those who respond to Luke's message know Jesus as Lord.

II. THE IMPLICATIONS

Scripture cannot contradict Scripture. Luke does not teach anything that contradicts John's message of eternal life through faith in Christ. If we read anything in Luke that seems to contradict John's message, then we have not understood what Luke is saying. We should not read Luke's teachings about discipleship into John's teaching of the free offer of eternal life.

John writes about what is required in order for someone to *become* a Christian. Luke writes about what is required of believers if they want to *live* as Christians, or followers, of Jesus Christ. The requirements are very different.

Understanding this will help the exegete, as the following examples show.

---

[3] Alberto Valdés, "Luke," in *The Grace New Testament Commentary,* ed. Robert N. Wilkin (Denton, TX: Grace Evangelical Society, 2019), 114.

[4] Robert N. Wilkin, "John," in *The Grace New Testament Commentary,* ed. Robert N. Wilkin (Denton, TX: Grace Evangelical Society, 2019), 177.

A. The Sermon on the Plain (Luke 6:20-49)

In this sermon, the Lord issues several commands. He addresses those who are on the inside, His disciples. He is not explaining how to become a Christian, but what He expects of His followers. At no point is there any hint or suggestion that failure to follow His commands means they were never born again or that they have lost their salvation. The ideal disciple is willing for the Lord to train him so that he becomes more and more like his Lord (v 40).

Luke makes it clear in his Gospel, addressed to the community of faith, that the training process is rigorous. This rigorous training is a requirement for being a disciple of the Lord Jesus and becoming His follower.[5] It is not required to receive eternal life by becoming a believer in Christ. Explaining how to receive eternal life is the purpose of John's Gospel.

B. The Free Gift and the Costly Tower

One passage in John and another in Luke are good examples of the two books' different purposes. They show the difference between receiving eternal salvation and being a disciple. In John 4, the Lord tells a woman at a well what she needs to do in order to receive the gift of eternal life. In Luke 14, Jesus teaches His disciples what they need to do in order to follow Him. One passage speaks of what is free, the other of something very costly. They cannot be talking about the same thing.

In John 4:10, Jesus tells the woman that He has a gift to offer her. She is an unbeliever. She does not have to do anything to receive the gift. She simply needs to know—to believe—who He is and what His gift is.[6] The gift is eternal life that can never end.

In Luke 14:28-30, the Lord speaks to His disciples metaphorically about building a tower. The tower represents the life of a disciple. Giving one's life in service to the Lord is very costly, as is building a tower. The disciple needs to count the cost. This verse, and those that immediately follow, show that the requirements for being a follower of Christ are costly. He compares it to going to war. The Lord makes it clear that if we do not meet the requirements, we do not qualify as His

---

[5] Stein is an example of one who confuses salvation and discipleship. See, Robert H. Stein, *Luke,* The New American Commentary (Nashville, TN: Broadman & Holman, 1992), 215.

[6] Zane C. Hodges, *Absolutely Free! A Biblical Reply to Lordship Salvation* (Dallas, TX: Redención Viva, 1989), 40-42.

disciples, even though we have eternal life. Becoming a believer is free. Being a disciple is not.[7]

III. JOHN 2:23

If we keep in mind the differences between Luke and John, we can avoid the mistakes that many make when they interpret a verse like John 2:23:

> Now, when He was in Jerusalem at the Passover, during the feast, many believed in His Name when they saw the signs which He did. But Jesus did not commit Himself to them, because He knew all men (vv 23-24a).

Unfortunately, it is common for exegetes to take the requirements for discipleship, which is the emphasis in Luke, and read them into John 2:23. Such exegetes forget John's audience and purpose. They forget that eternal life is a free gift.

A. Introduction

A few years ago, in the Sunday school class I attend, one of our teachers began his class

with John 2:23-25. Almost immediately, a woman sitting toward the back of the class

said, in a whisper loud enough to be heard by most of the thirty to forty people present,

"Yes, but did they really believe?"

I have been thinking about her question. Most exegetes ask the same question and respond in the negative. They maintain that these people did not "really" believe. However, the Scripture itself states that they did believe. The verse uses the same terminology used in John 1:12:

> But as many as received Him, to them He gave the right to become children of God, to those who believe in His name.

[7] Martin appears to see a difference between being a believer and a disciple in this passage. John A. Martin, "Luke," in *The Bible Knowledge Commentary*, eds. J. F. Walvoord and R. B. Zuck (Wheaton, IL: Victor Books, 1985), 243-44.

The people in John 2:23 "believed in His name." According to John 1:12, they were children of God. From where, then, did the woman in our class get her question? Since Scripture gives such an unequivocal answer, one wonders why most interpreters say that these people did not believe.

Their answer should grieve us. We have been taught by Christian teachers—unwittingly, no doubt—to question the truthfulness of God's Word. We have been taught to doubt that God's Word means what it says.

B. Some Examples

The notion that those who believed did not "really" believe has a long history. In 1885, Alvah Hovey said that those in v 23 were not believers. He maintained that v 24 "affords proof…that the Evangelist did not mean to ascribe saving faith to the many spoken of in verse 23." Even though they believed, it was not a faith that would save them. They did not have eternal life. Hovey says that their faith "was mere belief on the ground of evidence, implying no radical change of character."[8] According to this view, there was something deficient in the faith of those John mentions in v 23.

Hovey is confused about the distinction between eternal salvation by faith alone and the concept of discipleship. A "radical change of character" is part of the discipleship process. It is not a requirement for believing in the free offer of eternal life. Believing in His name for eternal life is not synonymous with changing one's lifestyle.

John 1:12 says that these people were eternally saved and were the children of God. John 2:23 says they believed. Hovey says they did not, thus planting the seed of doubt in our minds and implying that God's Word does not mean what it plainly says.

Blum's commentary on John is a modern example of confusing discipleship and eternal salvation. Concerning John 2:23, he writes:

> The effect of these miracles…was to elicit faith on the part of many people. They believed in His name, that is, they trusted in Him. This was not necessarily saving faith as the next verse implies…Jesus knew that

---

[8] Alvah Hovey, "John," in *The Complete Commentary of the New Testament* (Philadelphia, PA: American Baptist Publication Society, 1885), 93.

> a temporary excitement or a faith based on signs was not sufficient.[9]

As in Hovey's commentary, Blum states that v 24 indicates that the people in v 23 did not believe. Their faith was not sufficient. It is presumptuous for Blum to claim that he knows what Jesus knew when the Scriptures do not indicate in any way that this is what Jesus was thinking.

Blum says the response of these people sprang from a "temporary excitement." But the verse itself says nothing about this faith being temporary in nature. Nor does it say they believed merely because they were excited. John calls their response *faith*.

In addition, Blum has redefined what "believe in His name" means. In John 1:12, to believe in His name is sufficient for salvation. But according to Blum's interpretation of 2:23, to believe in His name is not sufficient. On what authority does he offer this new and awkward definition? It is not on the authority of Scripture, but on his own. He puts us in the position of not being able to understand the Bible unless we read his commentary alongside it. This requires that we trust him rather than what the Word of God clearly says.

What do the Scriptures say about the people in John 2:23? If we allow John 2:23 to speak for itself, we can very safely conclude that they were baby Christians. The Passover celebration lasted for seven days. If someone believed in Him on the first day of Passover, and this was the last day of Passover, he would have been a believer for just one week. We would not call the faith of a week-old Christian a "temporary excitement." We would not call it an insufficient faith. The faith of a new believer is still faith.

Both Blum and Hovey refer to "a faith based on signs." They see such a faith as problematic. In fact, they say that such a faith is not faith. According to them, a faith based upon signs is not a saving faith. However, in his purpose statement, the apostle John writes that Jesus performed the signs so that the unbelieving reader might read about them and believe in Him for eternal life (John 20:30-31). John did not consider a faith based on signs to be a deficient faith.[10] It appears that Blum has a higher standard for faith than God does.

---

[9] Edwin A. Blum, "John," in *The Bible Knowledge Commentary*, eds. J. F. Walvoord and R. B. Zuck (Wheaton, IL: Victor Books, 1985), 280.

[10] Wilkin, "John," 233.

Note as well that Blum says v 24 "implies" that the faith in v 23 is not saving faith. But v 24 implies nothing of the kind. Instead, the idea that the faith in v 23 is not saving faith is an inference that Blum has read into the text based on his confused theology.

Both Blum and Hovey feel the tension between v 23 and v 24. But the correct explanation of that tension is found in the distinction between salvation and discipleship. The tension is not removed by redefining *faith*.

Blum has confused apples with oranges. An *implication* arises directly from the text itself and is an integral part of the text's inspired meaning. An *inference* is an idea that the reader concludes from the text. An inference is not a part of the text's meaning, but it can be a valid extension of the meaning. Or it can be a non sequitur. When Blum infers that v 24 indicates the faith in v 23 is non-saving faith, his inference is not a valid conclusion but a non sequitur. Why? Because he says v 24 makes v 23 mean the opposite of what it actually says, thereby making Scripture contradict Scripture.

Blum writes, "Until His death and resurrection and the coming of the Holy Spirit, the foundation for faith was not fully laid."[11] This suggests that prior to the Day of Pentecost in Acts 2, there was something deficient in the faith of all the people of God.

The idea that the Bible teaches we can believe in Jesus yet not be saved dates back in the commentary tradition to at least the 19th century, as evidenced by Hovey. Both Hovey and Blum view the faith of those in v 23 as nonexistent, despite the fact that the text states it exists. Once again, the seeds of doubt are sown in our minds. God's Word does not mean what it says, and we cannot possibly understand its meaning without the aid of theologians.

Another modern example should be cited. Bruce, in discussing the faith of those in v 23, says, "There are two levels of believing in Jesus' name—that spoken of in John 1:12, which carried with it the authority to become God's children, and that spoken of here."[12]

Though the language of v 23 is identical to the language of 1:12, Bruce says those who believed in v 23 were only "superficially impressed because they saw the bare signs."[13] In other words, there was something

---

[11] Blum, "John," 280.

[12] F. F. Bruce, *The Gospel of John* (Grand Rapids, MI: Eerdmans, 1983,), 78.

[13] Ibid., 77.

deficient in their faith. Bruce is not saying there are two levels of faith; he is saying the faith in 2:23 is **not** faith.

With virtually no textual support, Bruce, Blum, and Hovey conclude that the faith of those who believed in v 23 was not saving faith. All three indicate that a faith based on signs is deficient. These three commentators say that those in v 23 did not *really* believe.

I have used these three examples because they reflect the view of most theologians. If they had been in the Sunday school class when the woman asked the question, "Did they really believe?" they would have answered, "No!"

IV. HOW DO WE RESPOND?

Hovey, Blum, and Bruce have the weight of scholarly opinion on their side. It is challenging to go against such a prevailing trend. How should we view that opinion?

We should let the Scriptures speak for themselves. John says that the people in v 23 believed. Since God inspired his writings, that is what God said. Since most commentators say that the people in v 23 did not really believe, they are disagreeing with God. Bruce says that there are two levels of believing in Jesus' name. He is misguidedly trying to rightly divide the Word of Truth (2 Tim 2:15). There are differences and distinctions in the Scriptures of which we need to be aware. However, Bruce's problem is that in saying there are two levels of faith—a faith in the name of Jesus that saves and a faith in the name of Jesus that does not—he is wrongly dividing the Word of Truth. He is not recognizing legitimate distinctions. He is saying that something means different things in different places.

We can appreciate that these theologians recognized a tension between vv 23 and 24. However, they failed in their effort to resolve that tension when they stated that the faith in v 23 was not genuine. They began with a faulty assumption when they attempted to understand v 24. They assumed that Jesus gives Himself to every believer.

When John says that Jesus did not *entrust* Himself to these believers, Hovey, Blum, and Bruce conclude that these people were not believers. They were not saved.

But the meaning of *entrust* can be found in the distinction between salvation and discipleship—a distinction we saw between the Gospels of John and Luke. In salvation, the issue is whether someone believes in Jesus. In discipleship, the question is whether Jesus can trust the one who has believed.

The account of the woman at the well in John 4 shows the distinction. She needs to know about the water Jesus offers her—the water that gives eternal life. The disciples, on the other hand, need to know about the food He offers. His food is to do the will of Him who sent Him.[14] He is speaking to those who have believed in Him for everlasting life and now claim to want to follow Him. Who among these will He be able to entrust with this work, doing the will of Him who sent Him? The disciples had already been part of the harvest, but can He now trust them (or us) to go back out into the field and bring the new harvest into the barn?

V. A BACKWARD METHODOLOGY

These three Evangelical teachers illustrate an all-too-common phenomenon: Too many scholars say that what the Scriptures call *faith* is deficient in some way. Hovey writes that the faith of those who saw Jesus perform signs "was *mere* belief on the ground of evidence." Blum, appealing to special knowledge of what Jesus knew—a special knowledge he does not possess—writes that though the people at the Passover believed in Jesus' name, their belief was not genuine and thus not salvific. And Bruce writes that what the Scripture calls *faith* in John 2:23 is deficient and "superficial" because it lacked commitment.[15] They all reflect a Reformed or Calvinistic view of faith: "Real" faith must be accompanied by good works. They are reading their theology back into John 2:23-24.

What are they teaching? They are teaching that we cannot trust the Word of God to mean what it says. Instead, to understand what the Bible is saying, we must read their commentaries.

What happened? These writers rightly felt a tension between John 2:23 and John 2:24. The people at the Passover believed in Jesus's name, but He did not believe in them. Rightly, we—like the three commentators referenced above—want to know how to resolve this tension. Hovey, Blum, and Bruce erred in their methodology. They started with v 24, assumed they knew what v 24 meant, then explained v 23 in light of their understanding of v 24. They worked backwards,

[14] Zane C. Hodges, *A Free Grace Primer* (Denton, TX: Grace Evangelical Society, 2018), 21-39.

[15] Hovey, "John," 93; Blum, "John," 28; Bruce, *John,* 78.

and this was the wrong direction. We know this because they made v 23 mean the opposite of what it plainly says.

A second problem with their method is that they explained a clear verse by looking at a difficult verse. The Bible, especially the Gospel of John, clearly states much about our belief in Jesus, but little about Jesus' belief in us.

VI. A BETTER WAY

There is a better exegetical method. To understand what John 2:23 means, we need to move from v 23 to v 24. This is moving from the clear to the less clear. Verse 23 says that "many believed in His name." John 1:12 gives us the theological significance of believing in the name of Jesus. To those who "believe in His name," Jesus confers the privilege of becoming the children of God. They are born from above (John 3:3).[16]

John 1:12 states the theology. John 2:23 gives the historical example. If we take the plain sense of John 2:23 and compare it with the theology of John 1:12, what would we conclude about the many at the Passover who believed in the name of Jesus? Assuming the authority of the Word of God and recognizing its reasonableness, we would not expect His Word to contradict itself. Based on John 1:12, we must conclude that the *many* of John 2:23 are, indeed, born of God. They are regenerate. They have experienced the new birth. If they had died, they would have gone to heaven. We will see them in heaven when we leave our bodies of flesh behind. They, along with all believers of all ages, will live in the kingdom of God, on the new earth, forever.

What, then, does v 24 mean? "But Jesus Himself did not entrust Himself to them for He knew all men." The *many* are brand new baby Christians. There is much that they must learn. They must be nurtured in this new life so they can grow and become useful in the Master's service. They are not yet ready for meat, but must first be nurtured on the milk of the Word. Spiritual growth is necessary in order for them to become trustworthy servants.

The apostle John has already given us a lesson in discipleship, just as he gave us a first lesson in the doctrine of regeneration. Earlier in chap. 2, John recounted the incident of Jesus' turning water into wine at the wedding in Cana. We learn what servants of Jesus are to do:

[16] Wilkin, "John," 180.

"Whatever He says to you, do it" (v 5). Jesus tells the servants at the wedding to fill the water pots, and they fill them to the brim. He tells them to draw out some of the water to take to the master of the feast, and they obey. John then makes the point that the master of the feast did not know where this great wine had come from, but "the servants who drew the water knew" (v 9).

It is those who have learned to serve the Lord who are privy to the secrets of the kingdom. If those who believed in His name in 2:23 were willing to learn from Him and how to follow Him, He would entrust more of Himself to them. And so it will be for all of us who seek to be the King's servants.

Hovey, Blum, and Bruce have illustrated a phenomenon that occurs far too often in Evangelical Christian circles: People who are considered Bible scholars often undermine the power and authority of the Word of God through eisegesis, which comes from the thinking of men rather than the Scriptures. Such twisted mis-explanations sow seeds of doubt in the minds and hearts of believers in Christ. Believers come to doubt their ability to understand the Scriptures for themselves. They think that the illuminating guidance of the Holy Spirit is insufficient. They can come to doubt that God's Word means what it says.

Let us hold fast to the sound Biblical traditions that we have been taught. Our Lord Jesus Christ, as the authorized and only Giver of the gift, offers the gift of everlasting life to anybody who "believes in His name."

Communicating that truth is the purpose of the Gospel of John. Let us not read the requirements of discipleship, which is the emphasis of Luke, back into a verse like John 2:23.

VII. CONCLUSION

There is one last thing we need to consider regarding the question: "Did they *really* believe?" That question is similar to one that was asked long ago: "Did God *really* say…?" (Gen 3:1).

In 1 John 4:6, the apostle John teaches us that we must rightly divide between the spirit of truth and the spirit of error. When these teachers listened to the seductive whisper, "*Did they really believe?*" they were listening to the same spirit of error whom Eve listened to in the garden many years long ago—a spirit who denied the truthfulness of God's Word then, and who denies the truthfulness of God's Word today. Did the people in John 2:23 really believe? God says they did. We will never be able to sort out the meaning of John 2:23-24 if we choose to assume that we know something more than God the Holy Spirit, who inspired John to write that they "believed in His name."

WHAT IS THE MAIN POINT OF ECCLESIASTES?[1]

BRAD DOSKOCIL

Long Beach, CA

I. INTRODUCTION

Ecclesiastes is an unusual book. There are many views regarding its central point. Many view the book as a cynical look at life. A common word in the book is the Hebrew "*ebel*." It is often translated as "vanity" and is seen as a summary of the book's main topic.

A popular Catholic commentary reflects this view of Ecclesiastes. It maintains that the phrase "vanity of vanities" sums up the theme of the book, even if it does not describe the "variety of tests that the author applies to life."[2]

In this article, I will challenge this standard view.

II. IS LIFE MEANINGLESS?

Protestant theologians often concur with the Catholic view just stated. They are confident that Ecclesiastes teaches that our worldly lives are meaningless. Glenn, for example, says that there is "little doubt about the theme of Ecclesiastes," and that the stated theme bookends Ecclesiastes since the author announces it at the beginning and end of the book (1:2; 12:8). He repeats his main idea throughout the book (1:14; 2:11, 17, 26, etc.). Glenn also points out that the author is called the "Teacher." The author declares everything in this life to be "meaningless," NIV's translation of the Hebrew word *hebel,* or "vanity," the translation used in KJV, RSV, and NASB.[3]

Wiersbe agrees, but rewords the theme in the form of a question. He says that the author, Solomon, states his theme in 1:1-3, a summary of which asks the question: "Is life really worth living?" The author

[1] Editor's Note: Lord willing, GES plans to publish a commentary on the OT at the end of 2026. This article is an example of the kind of information the commentary will contain.

[2] R. E. Brown, J. A. Fitzmyer, and R. E. Murphy, *The Jerome Biblical Commentary,* vol. 1 (Upper Saddle River, NJ: Prentice-Hall, 1996), 534-35.

[3] D. R. Glenn, "Ecclesiastes," in *The Bible Knowledge Commentary,* eds. R. B. Zuck and J. F. Walvoord (Wheaton, IL: Victor Books, 1985), 976.

looks at this life, which is full of mysteries and contradictions, and wonders whether the "endless toil" of existence is worth it. People toil all their lives, then die. After they die, somebody less worthy inherits their wealth, then wastes it. Solomon concludes that the best thing to do is to enjoy God's blessings today, fear Him, and keep His Word. Wiersbe adds that the NT helps make sense of Solomon's conclusions. Paul says that "our labor is not in vain in the Lord" (1 Cor 15:58).[4]

This pessimistic view of life is the primary reason Ecclesiastes is considered unusual. Garrett says that while this is shocking to many, such an honest outlook on life, when combined with NT teachings, can lead the unbeliever to consider the claims of Christ and His offer of eternal life. Garrett says:

> Christian readers, after they have shaken off the initial shock of reading Ecclesiastes, have often described it as a defense of the faith or even an evangelistic work. Ecclesiastes shows that many of the pursuits of life, including wealth, education, and power, do not really fulfill. In that way Ecclesiastes shows that life without God is meaningless and drives the reader to faith.[5]

As can be seen, many view the focus of Ecclesiastes as *vanity*, suggesting that life is meaningless. Such a despairing view of life should drive a person to God with the hope that eternity will be better than the present. In the meantime, enjoy the good things in life.

However, this view and similar ones fall short of explaining Solomon's purpose in writing the book.

III. WHAT WAS SOLOMON'S[6] PURPOSE IN WRITING?

Fortunately, Solomon tells us his purpose. He states it directly. He poses the question he seeks to answer, then states his conclusion. We do not need to wonder.

---

[4] Warren Wiersbe, *Wiersbe's Expository Outlines on the Old Testament* (Wheaton, IL: Victor Books, 1993), 246.

[5] D. A. Garrett, "The Poetic and Wisdom Books," in *Holman Concise Bible Commentary* (Brentwood, TN: B&H Publishers, 1998), 244.

[6] Solomon was the writer of Ecclesiastes, even though his name is not mentioned. The writer was king over Israel and reigned from Jerusalem (1:1, 12). He was also wise and wrote many proverbs (12:9). These descriptions fit only Solomon, for he was David's son, king of Israel, reigned from Jerusalem, and was wise (1 Kgs 4:29-34).

In Eccl 12:13 we read, "The conclusion of the matter when all has been heard is:

Fear God and keep His commands. This is for every man."[7]

In this final verse of the book, Solomon delivers the bottom line. This is reminiscent of John's placing his purpose in writing his Gospel at the end of the book (John 20:30-31). The conclusion is the final outcome. The *matter* is the question Solomon asked at the beginning of the book:

> "What profit is there to the man in all his toil which he toils under the sun?" (1:3)

Ecclesiastes 12:13 provides the answer. It is the main point of the book. Everything in the book points to this.

"When all has been heard" refers to all the discussion, evidence, inquiry, and debate about life. It includes everything that has been written in Ecclesiastes. A sage will search out wisdom and work tirelessly to discover truths, but when all the evidence is in, Solomon can say with assurance, "Listen to this!"

It boils down to two things. The first is to fear God. The second is to keep His commands. These are not suggestions, but commands.

To fear God incorporates several thoughts. *To fear* means to be afraid. It suggests a hierarchy. God is God, and we are His creation. Respect, reverence, and awe are included in the meaning. Respect is showing honor and esteem for God. Reverence is a combination of honor, respect, love, and devotion to God. Awe is the recognition of God's greatness. Certainly, worship or bowing down is also contemplated. It is recognizing who God is in relation to who we are, then responding accordingly.

Solomon does not tell us how to fear God. He simply says we should do it. Several elements are involved. It is impossible to please God without belief (Heb 11:6). When we believe God, we agree with Him and His way of thinking. When we believe God, we are persuaded that what He says is true.

We must have knowledge. We must know God. We must know who He is and what He thinks. Knowing requires a relationship. We become children of God by believing in Jesus for everlasting life. This establishes a relationship, allowing us to develop fellowship with Him. Only a child of God can get to know God personally.

---

[7] This is the author's own translation from the Hebrew text.

Worship is necessary. When we know God, we love and adore Him. We bow down to Him. We honor and praise Him.

We fear God by obeying Him. We keep His commands. We do what He tells us to do.

The NT combines the idea of love and obedience (John 14:1; 1 John 2:3). Jesus told the disciples that if they loved Him, they would keep His commandments. Love is not a feeling, but an action. The grace of God is a powerful incentive to obey what the Lord has commanded us (John 14:15).[8]

Knowing God is not to be equated with being a believer. Knowing Him refers to an intimate, personal knowledge of Him, and is a picture of fellowship. This would imply a love for Him. The believer who claims to know God in this way can test his claim. If it is true, he will keep God's commandments.[9]

In the OT, we can see these elements in one great example. Genesis 22:1-12 recounts Abraham and Isaac's journey to worship God. While there are many truths that can be drawn from this great passage, I am going to focus on what it means to fear God.

The account begins with Abraham's being available to God. When God called Abraham, he responded and said, "Here I am." God then gave Abraham an unusual instruction. He told him to go to the land of Moriah and offer Isaac, his only son, as a burnt offering. Abraham did not delay or argue about this unusual commandment. Rather, he quickly set out to do what God had told him.

When they arrived at the place, Abraham instructed his servants to stay with the donkeys while he and Isaac went up the hill to worship, then return. Abraham believed that both he and Isaac would return. Abraham believed the promise of God; obedience was therefore easy (Heb 11:17-19).[10] Abraham knew that if he offered Isaac as a burnt offering, God would raise him from the dead. Abraham was certain they would return together.

Abraham and Isaac went up and prepared the offering. Just as Abraham took his knife to slay Isaac, God called out to Abraham once

---

[8] Robert N. Wilkin, "The Gospel According to John," in *The Grace New Testament Commentary*, ed. Robert N. Wilkin (Denton, TX: Grace Evangelical Society, 2010), 445.

[9] Zane C. Hodges, "The First Epistle of John," in *The Grace New Testament Commentary*, ed. Robert N. Wilkin (Denton, TX: Grace Evangelical Society, 2010), 1198.

[10] Kenneth W. Yates, *Hebrews: Partners with Christ* (Denton, TX: Grace Evangelical Society, 2019), 183; J. Paul Tanner, "The Epistle to the Hebrews," in *The Grace New Testament Commentary*, ed. Robert N. Wilkin (Denton, TX: Grace Evangelical Society, 2010), 1082.

again. Abraham replied just as he had done before: "Here I am." Abraham was still available to God. God then makes a powerful statement: "Do not stretch out your hand against the lad, and do nothing to him; for now I know that you fear God, since you have not withheld your son, your only son, from Me" (Gen 22:12). Here is acknowledgement of a person who feared God, from God Himself!

This entire episode exemplifies belief, knowledge, worship, and unquestioning obedience. Abraham feared God. We know because God told him so!

To keep God's commands simply means to obey His commands. There are plenty of dos and don'ts in the Bible! However, there are different commands for different people or groups of people. There are also commands that relate to different time periods. Understanding the Bible is therefore necessary to determine which commands to obey and when to obey them.

Solomon ends Ecclesiastes with a universal application. His conclusion applies to everyone! There are no exceptions. Everyone should fear God and obey His commands. Solomon explains why this is important in the final verse:

> "For God will bring to judgment every work, including all that is concealed, whether good or bad" (Eccl 12:14).[11]

IV. ETERNAL REWARDS PLAY A MAJOR ROLE

Solomon explains why his conclusion has a universal scope. God is going to judge every human work. God is not going to miss any works. He has a perfect record-keeping system that records everyone's works. Every work will be evaluated.

When does God judge every work done by mankind? Logically, this can occur only after human history has ended; otherwise, how could God judge all human works? Solomon has already observed instances in which people do things and are not held accountable, so in this life, judgment of every work is improbable.

Some suggest that it is doubtful that Solomon is talking about future judgment after death because Solomon would not have been familiar with such a notion.[12] This contradicts Solomon's statement

[11] This is the author's own translation from the Hebrew text.

[12] Glenn, "Ecclesiastes"; electronic version accessed via Logos 8 Bible Software.

and assumes that the idea of judgment of works for the purpose of rewards is not an OT teaching.

However, Hebrews 11 refutes this assumption.[13] In that chapter, numerous OT heroes of faith are described as seeking reward for their faithful service. Terms such as *heir*, *inheritance*, *reward*, *gained approval*, and *received a better resurrection* are used. Hebrews 11 is a review of OT heroes who endured hardship in order to gain approval and receive eternal rewards.

Solomon also understood the concept of eternal rewards. This is obvious in Ecclesiastes. At the beginning of the book, he asks, "What profit (reward) is there for a man in all his toil or work?"

In the future, God will judge all human works. Every person will be evaluated (Heb 9:27). Contrary to the claim of those who teach that there is one final judgment, solely for the purpose of determining who goes to heaven, the Bible presents two separate judgments based on human works. One judgment is for believers; the other is for unbelievers. One is for those who have everlasting life; the other is for those who do not. One judgment is for saints; the other is for those who are not.

For believers, this judgment—the Judgment Seat of Christ—occurs when Jesus returns to earth to establish His earthly kingdom (Matt 16:27; Luke 14:14; 2 Tim 2:12; Rev 2:26-27; 3:21; 20:4-6). The judgment of unbelievers—the Great White Throne Judgment—happens after Jesus' thousand-year reign on earth (Rev 20:11-15). It is at these two judgments that mankind's works will be judged.[14]

What is the purpose of these judgments? It is related to mankind's original responsibility given by God. Mankind was charged with ruling over the earth (Gen 1:26-31; 3:19). That was man's job! Man was to keep the place in order. God holds His creatures accountable for the jobs assigned to them. Notice that works and the judgment of works have nothing to do with obtaining everlasting life. Rather, the evaluation is about compensation for work that is done well and that has value to the Creator. Jesus is fair. He pays His workers for their service to Him.

---

[13] See Yates's discussion of Chapter 11 in *Hebrews: Partners with Christ,* and Tanner in "Hebrews."

[14] Even though they are not mentioned in the NT, it can be assumed that people who come to faith during the millennial kingdom will have their works judged at the end of the 1,000 years. Believers before the coming of Christ will either be judged at the Judgment Seat of Christ or will have their own, separate judgment to determine rewards before the beginning of Christ's kingdom.

The judgment for believers includes all that is concealed or hidden. People do works that no one else sees. They are not apparent to others. They are anonymous. Jesus taught about secret works in Matt 6:1-7 and 16-17. Jesus is fair. He takes these unseen works into account. Jesus, the perfect Judge, knows all the facts and weighs them.

This judgment for believers will also examine both good and bad works (2 Cor 5:10). This acknowledges that not all work supposedly done for the Lord is commendable. Some work is good, and some work is bad. Not all work done in Jesus' name will be rewarded. Jesus does not pay His employees for simply showing up for work. The work must have value to Him. This is a challenge to each of us. Are the things we do to please the Lord things that He values?

At the Judgment Seat of Christ, Jesus will review every believer's works to determine their value to Him and to pay the believer accordingly. This judgment is about eternal reward, or treasure in heaven. It also forms the basis for Jesus' government in His earthly kingdom. He will promote some who will then rule and reign with Him. There is great honor and joy in being rewarded and even more in ruling with Jesus.

Abraham's actions regarding Isaac in Genesis 22 will be rewarded. Hebrews 11 bears that out. In Ecclesiastes, Solomon teaches the same thing.

V. THE JUDGMENT OF UNBELIEVERS' WORKS

The Great White Throne judgment is a judgment exclusively for unbelievers. Those who appear before Jesus at this judgment are "dead." This means that they do not have everlasting life (John 5:24). They never believed in Jesus for everlasting life.

Works are also judged at this judgment. The unbeliever is given the chance to present his case to Jesus. He will argue that he did good works and that he is a good person. He thinks his good works will merit entrance into Jesus' eternal kingdom (Matt 7:15-23). However, the works are dismissed and considered of no value to the Judge. They may have been done in His name, but were not done within a relationship to Him.[15] Instead, Jesus checks the birth records in the Book of Life

---

[15] Jesus fulfills the command of Gen 1:26-31 to rule over the earth. The first Adam failed. The second Adam does not. Therefore, in order to participate in Jesus' reign, people must be identified with Him. Jesus rewards work done by members of His own team. Unbelievers are still

to see whether any of those standing before Him have a spiritual birth certificate. The question is: "Do they have everlasting life?" The answer comes back: "I never knew you." They have no relationship to Jesus. They do not have a spiritual birth certificate. They do not have everlasting life. Consequently, they are banished to the lake of fire forever.[16]

This event is like a person trying to enter a country. He is at the border crossing. The border agent asks to see the person's passport. The person has no passport but instead presents his accomplishments and good works done on behalf of the country. He reasons, "You have to let me in because of all the great things I have done for your country!" The border agent turns him away. He has no passport. He cannot prove his citizenship, because it does not exist.

VI. CONCLUDING THOUGHTS

When did Solomon write Ecclesiastes?

Solomon authored several books of the Bible: Proverbs, Song of Songs, and Ecclesiastes. He also wrote Psalms 72 and 127. The traditional Jewish belief is that Solomon wrote the Song of Songs in his youth, Proverbs in his maturity, and Ecclesiastes at the end of his forty-year reign, around 940 BC (2 Chron 9:30).

The contents of Ecclesiastes show the writer as he reflects back on his life and experiences. We would therefore expect the writer to be old and near the end of his life. Solomon was an idolater at the end of his life, prompting God to pronounce judgment on him (1 Kgs 11:1-8). God appeared to Solomon and told him that his kingdom would be taken away (1 Kgs 11:9-13).

Solomon likely wrote Ecclesiastes after God appeared to him. God's judgment prompted Solomon to examine in a debater's fashion the fact that God judges everyone's works and that eternal rewards can be lost.

Looking back on his own life, Solomon realized the importance of obeying God. We know from 1 Kgs 11:9-13 that Solomon's life did not end well. God told him that his empire was going to be ripped apart. To use Solomon's own words, his empire was going to become a *vapor*!

---

identified with Adam, and so are on the wrong team. Consequently, their works have no value to Jesus. Matthew 7:15-23 bears this out.

[16] Hal M. Haller Jr., "The Gospel According to Matthew," in *The Grace New Testament Commentary*, ed. Robert N. Wilkin (Denton, TX: Grace Evangelical Society, 2010), 36.

That God appeared to Solomon and rebuked him may have prompted him to reflect on his life, leading him to write Ecclesiastes. Solomon had drifted away from God and become an apostate. His life accomplishments were about building his own empire, which God dismantled when Rehoboam took over. Perhaps Solomon reflected on his own eternal significance and—being wise and honest—wrote Ecclesiastes. In the end, the prospect of being judged by God may have caused Solomon to fear God.

The Book of Ecclesiastes is the one OT book that contrasts rewards in this life with eternal rewards. The doctrine of eternal rewards should cause the reader to reject the common way of understanding the book. It is not a pessimistic view of life. Anyone who reads this book should realize that human accomplishment is fleeting unless it is achieved while fearing God and obeying His commands.

THE CARROT OR THE STICK? A NEUROPHYSIOLOGICAL AND THEOLOGICAL APPROACH TO SUSTAINED ETERNAL FOCUS

ELLIE STEVENS STRATHMAN, D.O.

Board Certified Psychiatrist

I. INTRODUCTION

The doctrine of eternal rewards as distinct from eternal salvation (Eph 2:8-9), is a neglected teaching in many churches. Eternal rewards are *eternal incentives and opportunities* that God promises those who follow Him and are faithful to Him. Eternal life (regeneration) is given to those who believe—who are convinced—that Jesus gives everlasting life to anyone who believes in Him for it (John 6:47). By conflating eternal rewards and regeneration, many teachers and pastors negate the significance and emphasis placed on eternal rewards throughout Scripture.

For example, Craig Blomberg states:

> I do not believe there is a single NT text that, when correctly interpreted, supports the notion that believers will be distinguished one from another for all eternity on the basis of their works as Christians. What is more, I am convinced that when this unfounded doctrine of degrees of reward in heaven is acted upon consistently—though, fortunately, it often is not—it can have highly damaging consequences for the motivation and psychology of living the Christian life.[1]

This quote exemplifies a common theological perspective on the topic of eternal rewards. Blomberg cites psychology to support his argument, but provides no clinical or medical data to substantiate his claim. This article will refute the claim made by scholars such as Blomberg by showing that there are connections between Biblical teachings and cognitive neuroscience. I will argue that eternal rewards optimize neuropsychological and neurophysiological processes, enhancing one's

---

[1] Craig Blomberg, "Degrees of Reward in the Kingdom of Heaven?," *JETS* 35 (June 1992): 160.

ability to self-regulate—control one's emotions and behavior—and to make sound decisions, thus refuting Blomberg's claim that the teaching of eternal rewards can have damaging consequences for Christians.

First, I will examine Biblical evidence for eternal rewards. Next, I will present neuroscience research on reward-driven attention, contextual cueing, and delayed gratification. Finally, I will apply these findings to Christian living, demonstrating their alignment with Scripture.

Eternal rewards are intended for every believer, though not every believer will pursue or obtain them. They are indeed an extra incentive when the going gets tough. They are that firm hope awaiting us when we feel like giving in or giving up. They are the vindication we look forward to in the midst of persecution. However, there is more to eternal rewards than long-term reward. There is also a temporal benefit.

Rewards produce a refining and reinforcing effect through every circumstance of our lives. An eternal focus is necessary not only in negative circumstances but also when things are going well. In this article, I will outline how our brains are primed to seek and pursue reward through cognitive neuroscience. I will discuss how research indicates that specific areas of the brain, such as the prefrontal cortex (PFC), play a crucial role in executive function, self-regulation, and decision making. These functions are enhanced through delayed gratification, which encapsulates the doctrine of eternal rewards.[2] Living life by avoiding consequences and fearing punishment draws on the more primitive areas of our brains. Future-focused, high-value pursuits draw on the higher-functioning areas.

This concept, known as the "hot/cool framework," is reflected in Walter Mischel's research, which will be discussed later. It is a neurocognitive model that demonstrates the contrast between the impulsive (hot) process and the deliberate (cool) process of decision-making. The cool framework is characterized as a system that is well-adapted and that utilizes reflective, deliberate, and goal-driven processing, versus the hot framework, which is an emotional system that is reactive and impulsive. The cool framework is governed by the brain's prefrontal cortex (PFC), which inhibits impulses and is responsible for higher cognitive functioning, self-regulation, and decision-making. The hot framework is categorized by activation of limbic structures

---

[2] Vivian Zayas, Walter Mischel, and Gayathri Pandey, "Mind and Brain in Delay of Gratification," in *The Neuroscience of Risky Decision Making* (Washington: American Psychological Association, 2014), 153, https://doi.org/10.1037/14322-007.

(involved in emotions), and the amygdala (which can promote fear and anger).[3] The more one inhibits impulses and reactivity, thereby delaying immediate gratification, the more he strengthens the cool framework and operates in a well-adapted and goal-oriented way.

II. BIBLICAL BASIS FOR ETERNAL REWARDS

Eternal salvation is a gift freely given to those who believe in Jesus for eternal life (John 3:16; John 6:47; Eph 2:8-9), while eternal rewards are incentives for faithful discipleship (Rev 22:12; 2 Tim 4:8). Knowing that God will reward us for our suffering produces a healthy perseverance that the apostle Paul describes in 2 Cor 4:16-19:

> Therefore, we do not lose heart. Even though our outward man is perishing, yet the inward man is being renewed day by day. For our light affliction, which is but for a moment, is working for us a far more exceeding and eternal weight of glory, while we do not look at the things which are seen, but at the things which are not seen. For the things which are seen are temporary, but the things which are not seen are eternal.

Eternal rewards shift one's focus to eternal opportunities while optimizing our brains to produce a neural efficiency (optimal structural and functional use of cognitive resources) stemming from the PFC, thus enhancing self-regulation.[4] This aligns with what Jesus was teaching when He said, "For My yoke is easy and My burden is light" (Matt 11:30). Legalism, which incurs a difficult yoke and heavy burden, promotes the seeking of emotional rewards such as security, approval, and external validation. The concept of eternal rewards, by contrast, focuses on reflective pursuit—an easy yoke and light burden—rather than rigid conformity.

The apostle Paul addressed the issue of legalism in his epistle to the church at Galatia. In Gal 5:1, he explicitly wrote about the liberty that believers have in Christ. In 5:5, he wrote about the hope of righteousness by faith that he and other believers are waiting for. The imputed righteousness that believers receive at the moment of regeneration is

---

[3] Ibid., 152-53.

[4] Adrian Curtin et al., "Enhancing Neural Efficiency of Cognitive Processing Speed via Training and Neurostimulation: An fNIRS and TMS Study," *NeuroImage* 198 (September 2019): 74, https://doi.org/10.1016/j.neuroimage.2019.05.020.

not something they are waiting for. They already have it (Rom 3:22). Liberty and walking by the Spirit—the theme of Galatians—is lived out when a believer focuses on Jesus Himself and the reward that He has in store for those who are faithful. This liberty and empowerment by the Holy Spirit oppose legalism, comparison, and pride, and help believers love and serve one another (Gal 5:13, 25-26).

The term *disciple* means "follower." As we follow and imitate Jesus, we are conformed to His likeness. The Holy Spirit guides this transformation as we "behold the glory of the Lord" (2 Cor 3:18). Beholding the glory of the Lord is not automatic. It takes discipline, sacrifice, perseverance, and the pursuit of "the knowledge of the glory of God in the face of Jesus Christ" (2 Cor 4:6). We cannot follow Jesus if our pursuit or focus is not on Him and His teachings, including those found in Matthew 6. Although it will involve suffering now, partaking in the glory of Jesus Christ when we see Him face-to-face will be well worth any struggles we face in this life.

Paul states in Rom 8:17 that we will be "joint heirs with Christ if indeed we suffer with Him, that we may be glorified together." This differs from simply being *children* and *heirs* of God, referred to earlier in the verse. If we want to be a part of this glory we behold and to experience this transformation, it will require persistent attention on Jesus and a focus on the eternal glory that He wants us to participate in.

The apostle Paul suffered immensely, yet he said, "For I consider that the sufferings of this present time are not worthy to be compared with the glory which shall be revealed in us" (Rom 8:18). Thus, Matthew 6 and other passages refute Blomberg's claim that teaching on eternal rewards leads to psychological harm. Instead, focusing on eternal rewards leads to Spirit-led self-regulation and brain optimization. Living a life in a generally cool framework is required in order to suffer well and to endure temptation, persecution, and loss. Jesus knew this and gave us an eternal rewards framework, along with the empowering of the Holy Spirit, to overcome those trials.

There are two reasons for why someone would reject this doctrine. First, failing to read and understand the context and misconstruing discipleship passages as evangelistic is an interpretive error. Second, a philosophical bias can lead to such rejection. For example, this bias is reflected by Blomberg's view that the doctrine has "highly damaging consequences for the motivation and psychology of living the Christian life."[5] However, to reject eternal rewards and make good works necessary for eternal life leads to fear-based, sub-optimal psychological health and well-being.[6] For example, Blomberg states that Paul was unsure of his eternal salvation and was striving to obtain it in:

> In 1 Cor 9:25, Paul compares our perseverance to the athlete striving for an Olympic crown. But unlike a race on a track in which there can be only one winner, "we" [Christians] all should compete for "the crown that will last forever." This "crown" is the same as the "prize" of vv. 24, 27, which one fails to receive if one is "disqualified" (adokimos)…Eternal life and death are at stake here, not gradations of reward.[7]

While Blomberg's view may discourage people due to his view that even the apostle Paul wasn't confident in his eternal destiny, 1 Cor 3:15 clarifies that eternal rewards are indeed distinct from eternal life. It is a rewards passage, stating that even the one who loses rewards is saved. Nothing in the immediate context of the passage suggests any discussion of eternal salvation; thus, it must be an eternal rewards discussion.

Matthew 6:19-24 emphasizes treasures in heaven as incentives for faithful discipleship, not for eternal salvation. This aligns with the flexible framework empowered by the Holy Spirit described in Gal 5:13-18, versus a rigid legalistic compliance. In 1 Cor 9:25, the verse on which Blomberg bases his argument, to be *disqualified* refers to loss of eternal rewards, not of eternal life.

In Matthew 6, Jesus first tells people that they should not seek the praise of others, but instead invest in the things of God. He then describes hypocrites, who act differently in public than they do in private, a concept expounded upon in the book of James. Jesus tells those who seek validation and praise from others in this life that they already have their reward (Matt 6:2). They are not awaiting the reward from God for a life of service to Him; instead, they are living for the earthly, immediately received reward. This perpetuates the hot framework and prevents optimal brain function and self-regulation,

---

[5] Blomberg, "Degrees of Reward in the Kingdom of Heaven?," 160.

[6] Elizabeth Stevens-Strathman, "To Fear or not to Fear? The Catastrophic Psychological Effects of Fear-based Theology, and the Liberating Impact of Eternal Rewards," JOTGES (Autumn 2024): 52.

[7] Blomberg, "Degrees of Reward in the Kingdom of Heaven?," 163.

just as frequently seeking likes on a Facebook or Instagram page does today.

Jesus goes on to command His followers to lay up treasures in heaven (Matt 6:19-20). He then says something that taps into the structure and function of the brain—something that no one at that time, other than Jesus, would have known:

> For where your treasure is, there your heart will be also. The lamp of the body is the eye. If therefore your eye is good, your whole body will be full of light. But if your eye is bad, your whole body will be full of darkness. If therefore the light that is in you is darkness, how great is that darkness! No one can serve two masters; for either he will hate the one and love the other, or else he will be loyal to the one and despise the other. You cannot serve God and mammon. (Matt 6:21-24)

Jesus' teaching here is related to the fact that our brains work to optimize and automate the pursuit of whatever we focus our time, treasure, and talents on. This is why the object of motivation is so critical. Whatever drives our lives is where we will end up. Whether we pursue eternal or temporal glory, our brains will focus on that object of motivation and pursue strategies to realize it. This is why we should focus on the Commander and not the commands. We focus on Jesus and pursue love for Him and others, and the Holy Spirit and our brains will help us sustain that focus.

In the Bible, we see forces competing for our attention. John wrote about this in 1 John 2:16: "For all that is in the world—the lust of the flesh, the lust of the eyes, and the pride of life—is not of the Father but is of the world." The brain's default is to seek out the easiest pleasure involving the least effort. What we can tangibly experience with our senses is often easier to pursue than what is more abstract or distant. In fact, our eyes are naturally equipped to seek tangible incentives, guided by oculomotor processes—those controlling eye movements—and subconscious mechanisms. This is why discipleship requires a lot of effort, focus, and accountability. Receiving eternal life is free through believing in Jesus Christ's promise; discipleship, however, is a costly yet transformative investment. However, when we work our brains in the right way, we optimize them for the hardest tasks. We optimize them to think critically and abstractly, applying God's wisdom while patiently enduring temptation and suffering under the most severe of attacks. Jesus knows better than anyone how to set His followers up for success and how to refine and prepare the body of Christ for His glory.

Having discussed the Biblical basis for eternal rewards, I will now turn to how neuropsychology is optimized through eternal rewards by enhancing self-regulation, thus refuting Blomberg's claim. While Blomberg and others seem to fear that rewards may promote unhealthy competition ("believers will be distinguished from one another for all eternity"), cognitive neuroscience suggests that rewards actually improve well-being and motivation by enhancing brain structures that optimize self-regulation, sound decision-making, and empathy. The goal of eternal rewards is not comparison and rivalry, but closeness with God. This has the opposite effect of unhealthy competition; instead, it aligns with a desire to serve God and others in order to obtain a deeper intimacy with Christ in the present and for eternity (Gal 6:3-5).

III. ETERNAL REWARDS: OPTIMIZING OUR PSYCHOLOGICAL WELL-BEING

We cannot serve both God and the world. We must choose one as our priority, and we must choose wisely, or we will squander our lives. I will discuss how psychological research illustrates this truth, beginning with what researchers have found regarding the importance of rewards in relation to what our brains attend to.

In a recent study, researchers discovered that the greater the reward we receive when the reward is paired with a specific stimulus, the more our focus and attention will be primed to look for that stimulus. The reward can be irrelevant to the tasks or goals we are actually pursuing, and can easily pull us off course if we are unaware of this effect.[8]

Incentives do not catch our attention simply because they stand out physically; our eyes are also naturally wired, through subconscious processes and eye movement control (oculomotor functions), to focus on incentives without our even realizing it. We have saccadic eye movement systems—"jerky" eye movements that help direct where our eyes look. These can be voluntary or reflexive. This is a powerful system. For example, researchers found that the possibility of a high monetary

---

[8] A. Bourgeois, L. Chelazzi, and P. Vuilleumier, "How Motivation and Reward Learning Modulate Selective Attention," in *Progress in Brain Research* (Elsevier, 2016), 229: 327, https://doi.org/10.1016/bs.pbr.2016.06.004.

return not only captures one's attention but also impacts saccadic eye movements, even to the point of overruling one's intentions.[9]

In other words, what one is incentivized by will prime one's brain and eyes to look at what will produce that reward, regardless of how irrelevant the information or object is to the goals one is consciously pursuing. When we focus on the things of this world and receive rewards in the form of earthly things, our attention becomes primed to focus on those things even more and to ignore other information or stimuli that are irrelevant to that earthly reward.

On the other hand, if, while we are focused on eternal rewards, some earthly rewards sneak in, we could easily be primed to focus on those earthly rewards. This can pull us off course if we let it. The beauty is that we have control over what we dwell on. Our eyes and brains can alert us to a reward, but we can decide whether or not to entertain that stimulus. This is done through higher-level brain structures, such as the PFC, that are optimized through delayed gratification, which we will discuss later.

We are creatures of habit, and unless we intentionally pursue a goal, our default will be to pursue the status quo.[10] The brain seeks to optimize efficiency and does not want to use more energy than necessary. It takes an outside intervention (reward) for the brain to move away from the status quo.[11]

This is why eternal rewards are so important. If we are not focused on Jesus Christ's glory and the glory we can share with Him, we will focus either on the things of this world or on a long list of restrictions and obligations. Either of these produces immediate gratification, whether through indulgences and pleasure or through the validation and pride that comes from "checking the boxes." Our brains will want to habituate us to this pursuit, with the result that the more immediate gratification we receive, the more satisfied we are with the status quo. Contrary to Blomberg's views, eternal rewards are necessary to promote a healthy and godly focus for Christian living.

---

[9] Jan Theeuwes and Artem V. Belopolsky, "Reward Grabs the Eye: Oculomotor Capture by Rewarding Stimuli," *Vision Research* 74 (December 2012): 83-84, https://doi.org/10.1016/j.visres.2012.07.024.

[10] Wendy Wood and Dennis Rünger, "Psychology of Habit," *Annual Review of Psychology* 67, no. 1 (January 2016): 294, https://doi.org/10.1146/annurev-psych-122414-033417.

[11] Ibid., 294

IV. GUIDED BY GRACE: HOW CONTEXTUAL CUEING SHAPES OUR FOCUS ON ETERNAL REWARDS

The optimization of psychological processes by eternal rewards sets the stage for understanding contextual cueing, a cognitive mechanism by which repeated environmental patterns enhance one's ability to pay attention outside conscious awareness. By guiding our attention through familiar environmental patterns, contextual cueing helps us to remain focused on eternal priorities, shaping how we perceive and pursue what holds lasting eternal significance.

In a recent study, participants were instructed to focus on specific stimuli and ignore others, and were highly rewarded for doing so. The more they were rewarded, the better they became at ignoring distractions and focusing on the relevant stimuli.[12] One can see a relationship between the contextual cueing process and the concept of discipline in the Christian life that is presented in Scripture. In Matt 6:21-24, Jesus was describing contextual cueing when He explained that an eternal focus directs one's attention toward that pursuit on a subconscious level.

This focus leads to a cool framework that optimizes decision-making and self-regulation. *Our brains subconsciously wire and reinforce the pursuit of what we value most.* On the one hand, if one pursues a rigid, legalistic approach, he focuses on avoiding negative behaviors and carrying out obligations without analyzing the situation or thinking critically. Those engaged in this type of pursuit seek instant validation and approval whenever they complete tasks. However, the motivation behind the tasks is not a close relationship with God, but an escape from eternal damnation or punishment. This fear-based way of life contributes to activation of the amygdala (an area of the brain that, when overactive, produces a fear response) and underactivation of areas of the PFC.[13] This, in turn, prioritizes emotions and impulse over self-regulation and reflective decision-making. The contextual cueing alerts individuals to living life by following a list of rules in an attempt to avoid punishment.

---

[12] Bourgeois, Chelazzi, and Vuilleumier, "How Motivation and Reward Learning Modulate Selective Attention," 327.

[13] Stephen Maren and Andrew Holmes, "Stress and Fear Extinction," *Neuropsychopharmacology* 41, no. 1 (January 2016): 64, https://doi.org/10.1038/npp.2015.180.

On the other hand, a mindset focused on eternal rewards establishes a semi-flexible routine, and this general structure allows for more creativity, empathy, and better discernment. This allows one to make decisions "in the gray" instead of requiring a set of concrete rules to follow. The contextual cueing centers on pursuing eternal rewards by following Jesus and optimizing one's relationship with Him. As one focuses on eternal things and minimizes distraction, the discipline required will become more of a semi-flexible routine that prioritizes the pursuit of eternal things. This routine enables greater cognitive flexibility, allowing resources to be allocated to other tasks, such as minimizing earthly distractions. The inverse would be the legalistic approach, which essentially micromanages the brain's processes, relying more on external validation or immediate emotional security. The difference between a legalistic and an eternally focused approach is the difference between a fear-based, rigid compliance and an opportunity-based, flexible pursuit.

V. WAITING FOR ETERNITY: HOW DELAYED GRATIFICATION SHAPES OUR PURSUIT OF ETERNAL REWARDS

Focusing on eternal rewards is an example of delayed gratification. As we inhibit the immediate impulses to fulfill the lusts of the flesh, we delay gratification until the Judgment Seat of Christ. Research has shown that the higher the reward, the more proficient one will be at suppressing irrelevant material.[14] If we can reprogram our minds to perceive eternal rewards as an everlasting investment of unequaled value, then that value will far surpass any temporary incentive here on earth.

A beautiful aspect of God's creation is that His design of the human brain enables children as young as four to delay gratification. Studies conducted by Walter Mischel in the 1970s examined children aged four through six. Each child was put in a room and given a marshmallow. The researcher told the child that if he or she did not eat the marshmallow by the time he returned in fifteen minutes, he would give the child another marshmallow. The children who were innately

---

[14] Chiara Della Libera and Leonardo Chelazzi, "Learning to Attend and to Ignore Is a Matter of Gains and Losses," *Psychological Science* 20, no. 6 (June 2009): 778, https://doi.org/10.1111/j.1467-9280.2009.02360.x.

able to delay gratification employed several strategies to achieve this. All ignored the marshmallow (first strategy). Some children actually hid the marshmallow out of sight to diminish the power of the temptation. A third strategy was reconstruction, i.e., reappraising the appeal of the stimulus. For example, they would think of the marshmallow as something less appetizing, such as a cloud.

Those who were able to focus their attention on things other than the immediate reward (eating the marshmallow) were able to delay gratification for a longer time.

Delayed gratification can be innately easier for some than others. One's ability to delay gratification can be impacted by chronic stress, drugs, and brain injuries, but it can be improved by attentional control and self-regulation strategies.[15]

The marshmallow study led Mischel to develop the hot/cool framework, which the field of cognitive neuroscience has studied and refined. The more a person delays gratification, the cooler they run. In reality, a person alternates between running hot or cold throughout the day due to various stressors. However, as a general way of life, the brain is optimized and makes the best decisions when a person runs cool. They make reflective and strategic decisions rather than impulsive and emotionally driven ones.[16]

The hot/cool framework aligns with Jesus' teaching in Matt 6:21-24, which focuses on heavenly treasures and engages PFC-mediated control. Rather than causing psychological harm, as Blomberg claims, this optimizes one's attention for pursuing eternal rewards.

VI. WIRED FOR ETERNITY: HOW NEUROPHYSIOLOGY SHAPES OUR PURSUIT OF ETERNAL REWARDS

Identifying how the structures of the brain, such as the PFC, affect one's behavior brings us to the neuroscience of delayed gratification. Cognitive neuroscience is an interdisciplinary field that involves the interaction of the fields of cognitive psychology (the study of brain processes) and neurophysiology (the study of the nervous system and its mechanisms). The interaction of the hot and cool systems, as observed in cognitive neuroscience, is demonstrated by the following

---

[15] Zayas, Mischel, and Pandey, "Mind and Brain in Delay of Gratification," 155.

[16] Ibid., 152.

explanation of how our actions affect the function of our brains and vice versa:

> One can enable the cool system by shifting attention from something that will trigger the hot response, which helps prevent that object or thought from going into working memory. If it goes into working memory, one can use reappraisal to reframe it as neutral. This activates the cingulate and prefrontal cortex and disengages the amygdala, which is associated with threat and fear.[17]

Another key area of cognitive neuroscience is neuroplasticity, which is related to Hebbian theory, a theory originally presented in a paper by D.O. Hebb,[18] and summarized by Carla Shatz with the phrase, "What fires together, wires together."[19] When one performs an action, the structures activated for that function are enhanced. The more the action is performed, the stronger the synapses (connections) become.

As we explore the structures involved in delayed gratification, we find that the connections of these structures become strengthened and the ability to delay gratification becomes more refined and reinforced the more it is exercised. In other words, we have control over how our brains function and can optimize the brain's function to help us work toward goals.

This paper will focus on the main areas of the brain involved in delayed gratification. This is not an exhaustive discussion, but it addresses the most crucial areas.

A. Right Temporoparietal Junction (rTPJ)

The *right temporoparietal junction (rTPJ)* is an area of the brain that *promotes social cognition,* or how we make sense of others' thoughts and behaviors in social settings (theory of mind).[20] This area of the brain (rTPJ) is also involved in *directing one's attention to future rewards.*[21]

---

[17] Ibid., 154.

[18] D. O. Hebb, The Organization of Behavior: A Neuropsychological Theory (New York: Wiley, 1949), 70.

[19] Carla J. Shatz, "The Developing Brain," *Scientific American* (September 1992): 64.

[20] Alexander Soutschek et al., "The Right Temporoparietal Junction Enables Delay of Gratification by Allowing Decision Makers to Focus on Future Events," *PLOS Biology* 18, no. 8 (August 2020): 2, https://doi.org/10.1371/journal.pbio.3000800.

[21] Ibid., 8.

It directs the mind to envision one's future self and the value of the rewards to come. At the same time, it reinforces the ability for one to be others-focused. The thickness of the rTPJ increases with delayed gratification,[22] meaning that the more you practice delayed gratification, the more that part of your brain is strengthened. This perpetuates future thinking—more focus on future rewards and less focus on immediate gratification. Enhancing the function of the rTPJ through delayed gratification by focusing on the eternal enhances one's ability to empathize and to understand how one's actions impact others. This counters Blomberg's fears that eternal rewards will create harmful competition.

B. Dorsomedial Prefrontal Cortex (dmPFC)

The *dorsomedial prefrontal cortex (dmPFC)* is involved in delayed gratification (self-control), as well as in being able to see things from others' perspectives (empathy). A recent study found that the dmPFC enhances self-control through decreasing one's self-centered focus.[23] The dmPFC is also enhanced through social interaction, high-level abstract thinking, and construal.[24]

Thus, both the rTPJ and the dmPFC are strengthened through delayed gratification and are integral to navigating social settings and considering others' perspectives, rather than only one's own. Both of these areas enhance the brain's focus on the collective, as the rTPJ focuses on future rewards. Prayer activates the temporoparietal junction as well as the dmPFC, strengthening both self-regulation and the ability to empathize, refuting Blomberg's claim.[25]

---

[22] Marieta Pehlivanova et al., "Diminished Cortical Thickness Is Associated with Impulsive Choice in Adolescence," *The Journal of Neuroscience*; Bourgeois, Chelazzi, and Vuilleumier, "How Motivation and Reward Learning Modulate Selective Attention," 2.

[23] Chen Jin et al., "The Dorsomedial Prefrontal Cortex Promotes Self-Control by Inhibiting the Egocentric Perspective," *NeuroImage* 301 (November 2024): 8, https://doi.org/10.1016/j.neuroimage.2024.120879.

[24] Kris L. M. R. Baetens, Ning Ma, and Frank Van Overwalle, "The Dorsal Medial Prefrontal Cortex Is Recruited by High Construal of Non-Social Stimuli," *Frontiers in Behavioral Neuroscience* 11 (March 2017): 8, https://doi.org/10.3389/fnbeh.2017.00044.

[25] Uffe Schjoedt et al., "Highly Religious Participants Recruit Areas of Social Cognition in Personal Prayer," *Social Cognitive and Affective Neuroscience* 4, no. 2 (June 2009): 202, https://doi.org/10.1093/scan/nsn050.

C. Ventral Tegmental Area (VTA)

Delayed gratification affects the *ventral tegmental area (VTA)* dopaminergic neurons, which is an area of the brain important for reward processing.[26] Dopamine plays a crucial role in motivation and the reinforcement of learning. The more delayed the reward, the more the VTA will steadily release dopamine to promote the delay.[27] This links motivation driven by dopamine to positive cognitive outcomes, demonstrating again the error of Blomberg's claim that believing in eternal rewards can have "highly damaging consequences for the motivation and psychology of living the Christian life."[28]

Referring back to the hot/cool framework, the practice of self-regulation enhances one's ability to stay calm and focused, enabling the individual to stay in the cool framework with more frequency through the phenomenon of neuroplasticity.

If one is operating within the hot framework, they are motivated by surrounding temptations, and those immediate "rewards" reinforce their visual attention toward those temptations. The individual is reactive, impulsive, and unable to see long-term goals or intrinsic rewards. This reminds me of when, in his second epistle, Peter wrote that believers who seemed to be living life in what we call the *hot framework* were shortsighted, blind, and forgetful (2 Pet 1:9).

If one is operating within the cool framework, the risk of falling back into the hot framework is low, especially if the individual is engaged in a community that encourages the cool framework. In 2 Peter 2, the apostle encouraged the community of believers who were his audience to persevere in light of eternal rewards:

> Therefore, brethren, be even more diligent to make your call and election sure, for if you do these things you will never stumble; for so an entrance will be supplied to you abundantly into the everlasting kingdom of our Lord and Savior Jesus Christ. (2 Pet 1:10-11)

Insights from cognitive neuroscience shed new light on "putting one's body into submission" (1 Cor 9:27). By following God's Word, one can alter the pathways and neural networks of the brain, reinforcing

---

[26] Zilong Gao et al., "The Neural Basis of Delayed Gratification," *Science Advances* 7, no. 49 (n.d.): 1, https://doi.org/10.1126/sciadv.abg6611.

[27] Ibid., 8.

[28] Blomberg, "Degrees of Reward in the Kingdom of Heaven?," 160.

these pathways and making it easier to remain obedient and focus on the rewards to come. Walking by the Spirit is running cool. The flesh is not running the mind; rather, the mind is taking control over the flesh.

VII. APPLYING ETERNAL FOCUS IN EVERYDAY LIFE

How does this fit into the life of a follower of Christ? We can look at some of the different anatomical structures of the brain and see how their optimization can enhance our walk with Him. The prefrontal cortex—which involves decision-making, abstract thinking, strategizing, executing behavior, and impulse control—helps us analyze and strategically apply Scripture to our lives. The ventral tegmental area helps us persevere in trials as it slowly releases dopamine while we delay gratification. The anterior cingulate cortex is involved in error detection and conflict management, thus aiding in discernment. The right temporoparietal junction— involved with understanding and identifying the perspective of others—helps to optimize our role within the body of Christ through empathy, conflict mitigation, and encouragement of others.

The short-term benefit is that by operating more in the cool framework, one becomes wiser, more patient, and more self-controlled, thus optimizing brain function.

The long-term benefit is fully realizing one's sense of belonging and purpose as a fellow heir of Jesus Christ for eternity. In short, the cool framework is what it looks like when a believer walks by the Spirit in fellowship with God. Such a believer will still sin, but will have a support network of like-minded believers and will be quick to confess sin in order to stay on track.

We can develop an approach to sustained eternal focus based on both neurophysiology and theology. I would suggest five points:

1. *Pursue the truth.* Engage in studying and applying Scripture with a theologically sound group of believers in order to pursue the truth and enhance self-regulation and executive functioning. Regular Bible study and application with an open mind and the ability to self-reflect align with Rom 12:1-2 and enhance cognitive

control, promoting the cool framework through optimizing the PFC.[29]

2. *Optimize your environment.* Environmental cues impact one's focus, as seen through contextual cueing.[30] Research has shown that the brain will be primed to focus on whatever elicits the highest reward.[31] One can minimize temptations without legalistically imposing those boundaries on others. Surrounding oneself with others who exert self-regulation and are also pursuing things of eternal value can also promote the cool framework.[32]

3. *Optimize your physical health.* Physical health directly impacts neurophysiology. There are tangible ways to improve physical health in order to optimize the brain's function. For example, a study shows that 250 mg of caffeine can decrease blood flow to the brain by up to approximately 30%, so avoiding or limiting caffeine could improve brain function.[33] It is also important to prioritize good sleep, as poor sleep can contribute to emotional dysregulation.[34] Additionally, getting exercise can increase gray matter brain volume in areas critical for cognition, thereby combating dementia and the negative effects of aging.[35]

4. *Optimize your mental health.* It is important to prioritize mental health and get professional help when necessary. Untreated mood disorders, as well as anxiety,

---

[29] Zayas, Mischel, and Pandey, "Mind and Brain in Delay of Gratification," 165.

[30] Bourgeois, Chelazzi, and Vuilleumier, "How Motivation and Reward Learning Modulate Selective Attention," 330.

[31] Theeuwes and Belopolsky, "Reward Grabs the Eye," 82-83.

[32] Michelle R. vanDellen and Rick H. Hoyle, "Regulatory Accessibility and Social Influences on State Self-Control," *Personality and Social Psychology Bulletin* 36, no. 2 (February 2010): 255-56, https://doi.org/10.1177/0146167209356302.

[33] Oliver G. Cameron, Jack G. Modell, and M. Hariharan, "Caffeine and Human Cerebral Blood Flow: A Positron Emission Tomography Study," *Life Sciences* 47, no. 13 (January 1990): 1141, https://doi.org/10.1016/0024-3205(90)90174-P.

[34] Matthew P. Walker and Els Van Der Helm, "Overnight Therapy? The Role of Sleep in Emotional Brain Processing," *Psychological Bulletin* 135, no. 5 (2009): 744, https://doi.org/10.1037/a0016570.

[35] Cyrus A. Raji et al., "Longitudinal Relationships between Caloric Expenditure and Gray Matter in the Cardiovascular Health Study," *Journal of Alzheimer's Disease* 52, no. 2 (May 2016): 725-26, https://doi.org/10.3233/JAD-160057.

can perpetuate the hot framework.[36] Finding ways to enhance our mental health can also help us with eternal focus. Exercise, beyond its physical benefits, improves the function of our brains and our ability to sustain focus through increasing the dorsolateral prefrontal activation.[37]

5. *Regularly check your focus.* As seen from contextual cueing, if believers are not intentionally directing attention toward eternal goals, thus creating familiar environmental patterns that will guide attention subconsciously, the default will be that the world and the flesh will guide their attention.[38] Regularly assessing one's focus—through prayer and through studying and applying Scripture both individually and with other believers—counteracts distractions and strengthens cognitive control.[39] This practice fosters a pursuit of eternal rewards, free from legalistic pressures.

Believers who pursue optimal brain health by incorporating these strategies while pursuing eternal rewards will maximize their ability to "love the Lord your God with all your heart, with all your soul, and with all your mind" (Matt 22:37).

Contrary to Blomberg's view, eternal rewards are Biblically grounded and neurophysiologically optimizing because they align with Christian discipleship and enhance self-regulation. Our brains are wired to require a reward that surpasses the challenges, risks, and losses that come with following Jesus. The goal of ruling with Christ in His eternal kingdom optimizes our brains to maintain the perseverance that this entails. (2 Cor 4:16-18).

Pastors, teachers, and counselors would be wise to teach and encourage the pursuit of eternal rewards, leveraging insights from

---

[36] Zayas, Mischel, and Pandey, "Mind and Brain in Delay of Gratification," 156.

[37] Hiroki Yanagisawa et al., "Acute Moderate Exercise Elicits Increased Dorsolateral Prefrontal Activation and Improves Cognitive Performance with Stroop Test," *NeuroImage* 50, no. 4 (May 2010): 1708, https://doi.org/10.1016/j.neuroimage.2009.12.023.

[38] Zayas, Mischel, and Pandey, "Mind and Brain in Delay of Gratification," 151-52.

[39] Dimitrios Kapogiannis et al., "Cognitive and Neural Foundations of Religious Belief," *Proceedings of the National Academy of Sciences* 106, no. 12 (March 2009): 4878-79, https://doi.org/10.1073/pnas.0811717106; Nina P. Azari et al., "Neural Correlates of Religious Experience," *European Journal of Neuroscience* 13, no. 8 (April 2001): 1651, https://doi.org/10.1046/j.0953-816x.2001.01527.x.

neurophysiology that demonstrate how it optimizes Christian living. Everyone seeks purpose and meaning. One day, those who sacrificed for God will be rewarded with opportunities to serve Him and have a closeness with Him that others who choose worldly gratification will not have. Eternal rewards are not selfish, nor do they have "highly damaging consequences fo the motivation and psychology of living living the Christian life."[40] God has given us a framework of eternal rewards to optimize our brains and to help us align with His will (Heb 11:6). It should come as no surprise that, as our Creator, God expects us to live according to the way we were designed to respond. If we live a life of sacrificing and suffering well, we will be chosen to serve God in significant capacities for eternity. There is no scarcity of rewards and therefore no need for competition. Rather, there will be—for each and every one who pursues eternal rewards—ample opportunities to partner with Christ in His eternal kingdom (Heb 3:14).

[40] Blomberg, "Degrees of Reward in the Kingdom of Heaven?," 160.

ETERNAL REWARDS TEACHING IN THE OLD TESTAMENT

ROBERT N. WILKIN

Associate Editor
Journal of the Grace Evangelical Society
Denton, TX

I. INTRODUCTION

Did Adam and Eve know anything about eternal rewards? Most Free Grace people are convinced that they came to faith in Christ for everlasting life very shortly after they sinned (See Gen 3:15).

But did they believe that the service they performed for the Lord in this life would be rewarded in the life to come? What did subsequent generations believe? Did Enoch, in the seventh generation, believe in eternal rewards? Abraham in generation 20? Moses in generation 26? King David in generation 34?

II. THE KEY OLD TESTAMENT WORDS AND EXPRESSIONS

In the OT, with the exception of *inherit/inheritance,* the words used for *reward* are not specific to rewards in the life to come. God rewards or recompenses people for their deeds. That is true in this life. However, very few of the following verses limit God's recompense for deeds to that which is given out in this life.

Reward/Rewarded (*seker, slm*). See Job 34:11; Psalm 58:11; Prov 11:18; 13:13; Isa 62:11; Jer 31:16.

Recompense (*slm, gemul, natan*). See 2 Sam 19:36; Prov 11:31; 12:14; Ezek 11:21.

Reap (*qsr*). Typically associated with sowing (as in Gal 6:8). See Job 4:8 (negative reaping); Ps 126:5; Prov 22:8 (negative reaping); Hos 10:12.

Inherit/Inheritance (*yrs/nhl*). See Ps 25:13 (future inheritance of the earth); 37:9 (future inheritance of the earth); Prov 3:35 (future inheritance of glory).

Judgment (*mispat*). See Eccles 12:14 (God will bring every work into judgment.)

The various words used in the OT imply a concept of rewards to be given to us both here and now and in the life to come. Let us now examine some specific OT texts that suggest an understanding of eternal rewards.

III. KEY OLD TESTAMENT PASSAGES

A. Daniel 12:1-2:

> At that time Michael shall stand up, the great prince who stands watch over the sons of your people; and there shall be a time of trouble, such as never was since there was a nation, even to that time. And at that time your people shall be delivered, every one who is found written in the book. And many of those who sleep in the dust of the earth shall awake, some to everlasting life, some to shame and everlasting contempt. Those who are wise shall shine like the brightness of the firmament, and those who turn many to righteousness like the stars forever and ever.

This is one of the clearest OT texts on eternal rewards, though most commentators think the issue here is eternal destiny only, not eternal life and possible eternal rewards. J. Dwight Pentecost's comments in the *Bible Knowledge Commentary* represent what most Evangelical commentators say:

> Unbelieving Jews will be resurrected to shame and everlasting contempt and will not partake in the covenanted blessings. Jews, however, who believe the Messiah will be resurrected bodily to everlasting life and to positions of honor in Christ's millennial kingdom. Being glorified in the kingdom, they will shine like the brightness of the heavens. (Cf. Matt. 13:43, "Then the righteous will shine like the sun in the kingdom of their Father.") They will be wise, for

> they will trust in the Messiah even though it will result in their suffering.[1]

The problem with this view is that Daniel conditions shining "like the stars" upon being wise and turning many to righteousness. Not all OT believers (those who will be resurrected) or Tribulation believers who have died (who will also be resurrected) will be wise and will turn many to righteousness.

Daniel is talking about two different groups. All believers will be raised to everlasting life. But wise believers who have led many to righteousness will be raised to special fullness of everlasting life.

The Faithlife Study Bible suggests a close connection between the Suffering Servant of Isaiah 52–53 and these believers, who will also be suffering servants.

> In Hebrew, significant allusions to the Servant Song in Isa 52:13–53:12 are evident. These linguistic links reflect a conscious understanding of Isa 53 as a text about resurrection. Just as the Suffering Servant figure is resurrected and restored to a relationship with God, His people also will be resurrected and restored to a relationship with Him. The allusions serve to connect God's people in Dan 12:2-3 with the Suffering Servant, so that God's servant—Israel (the "people" in v. 1)—is resurrected. The concept of judgment also is implicit here, with some receiving eternal life and others eternal contempt. In Daniel, the servant who is resurrected represents a group of people ("the many"), whereas in Isa 53:10-11 the Resurrected Servant is an individual. In OT theology, the two are closely identified.[2]

A comparison of Dan 12:2-3 with Matt 13:43 and Rom 8:17b shows that the issue here is eternal rewards, not eternal destiny.

Commenting on Matt 13:43, Blomberg writes: "But he promises radiant glory for the 'righteous' (v. 43)—those who do God's will by becoming disciples of Christ."[3] While Blomberg thinks that all the wheat

---

[1] J. Dwight Pentecost, "Daniel" in *The Bible Knowledge Commentary*, eds. John F. Walvoord and Roy B. Zuck (Wheaton, IL: Victor Books, 1985), 1372-73).

[2] Barry, Mangum, Brown, et. al, *Faithlife Study Bible*, s.v. Dan 12:2-3, Lexham Press.

[3] Craig Blomberg, *Matthew*, New American Commentary (Nashville, TN: Broadman &

(believers) "do God's will" and are faithful disciples, that is not true. But his statement stands. This reward is for those who are righteous in their experience.

Lenski comments on Matt 13:43:

> The kingdom a moment ago called that of the Son of man, is now called that "of their Father," making all the righteous princes and inheritors of this kingdom ("sons," v. 38). When that glorious day arrives, then shall be fulfilled Isa. 52:1; 60:21; Rev. 22:14, 15, and many other promises.[4]

While Lenski seems to think this is true of all believers, it is not. Note that he sees a connection with Rev 22:14, which deals with eternal rewards.

Not all believers will wear white garments. Not all will shine like Moses did after he met with Jesus or like the Lord Jesus at the Mount of Transfiguration. The glorious appearance is a reward for faithful service.

Though Ferguson does not make it clear that he is speaking about eternal rewards, he does comment: "The wise (cf. 11:25) who have been faithful to God's word, despite shame and suffering, will be glorified (3)."[5]

B. Isaiah 40:10:

> Behold, the Lord GOD shall come with a strong hand, and His arm shall rule for Him; behold, *His reward is with Him,* and His work before Him (emphasis added).

Taken by itself, this verse might lead us to wonder whether Isaiah is talking about rewards in this life or in the life to come. But when we compare this to an NT verse that uses the same language, we can see that it relates to eternal rewards. In Rev 22:12 the Lord Jesus says, "And behold, I am coming quickly, and *My reward is with Me,* to give to every one according to his work" (emphasis added). Revelation 22:14 then lists two of the rewards: the right to enter the New Jerusalem by its gates and

---

Holman), 223.

[4] R. C. H. Lenski, *The Interpretation of Matthew's Gospel* (Minneapolis, MN: Augsburg Publishing House, 1961), 540-41.

[5] S. B. Ferguson, "Daniel," in *New Bible Commentary*, eds. Wenham, Motyer, Carson, and France (Westmont, IL: InterVarsity Press, 1994), 762.

the right to eat from the Tree of Life.

Surprisingly, most OT commentators do not mention the connection with Rev 22:12. However, some do. Jamieson, Fausset, and Brown comment: "work—or, 'recompense for his work'; rather, 'recompense which He gives for work' (Is 62:11; Rev 22:12),"[6]

Barnes writes:

> It will be assuredly applicable to him when he shall come to gather his people to himself in the great and last day, and the language before us is used with reference to that: 'And behold, I come quickly; and my reward is with me, to give every man according as his work shall be' (Rev. 22:12).[7]

Gill mentions that some see this as referring to Rev 22:12 and Christ's Second Coming, but he disagrees: "...but it is more agreeable to the context, which foretells the coming of John the Baptist, points out the ministers of the Gospel, and describes Christ in his office, as a shepherd feeding his flock, to understand it of his first coming..."[8]

Revelation 22:12 alludes to Isa 40:10; the reward spoken of is therefore eschatological.

C. Psalm: 1:6

> For the LORD knows the way of the righteous, but the way of the ungodly shall perish.

While this key psalm may be talking about blessings in this life only, there are strong indications that David is speaking of eternal blessings as well.

Most commentators understand this verse to be speaking about those who will be in the kingdom, as opposed to those who will be in the lake of fire. Wiersbe writes:

> There is a coming day of judgment, and the Lord, the Righteous Judge, will separate the wheat from the tares, the sheep from the goats, and the trees from the chaff, and no unbeliever will be able to stand in the

[6] Robert Jamieson, Andrew Robert Fausset, and David Brown, *Commentary Critical and Explanatory on the Whole Bible*, vol. 1 (Logos Research Systems, Inc., 1997), 474.

[7] Albert Barnes, *Notes on the Old Testament: Isaiah*, vol. 2 (London: Blackie & Son, 1851), 63.

[8] John Gill, *An Exposition of the Old Testament*, vol. 5 (London: Mathews and Leigh, 1810), 224.

> assembly of the righteous. The verb knows in verse 6 doesn't mean that God is aware of them intellectually and has the godly in his mind. Rather, it means that God has chosen them and providentially watched over them and brought them finally to His glory.[9]

Ross comments: "Salvation in the day of judgment is equated with being known by the Lord (cf. Matt. 7:23)."[10]

Ellsworth says, "Those who choose to live apart from God and his people in this life will find that they will have no part with them in eternity."[11]

The problem with this view is that it contradicts the promise of everlasting life to the believer found in over a hundred verses in the Bible, especially in the Gospel of John. If John 3:16 is true, then Ps 1:6 is talking about eternal rewards, not eternal destiny, since in this psalm, *the righteous* are clearly those who live righteously, and *the ungodly* are those who live unrighteously.

Here is what I have written concerning Ps 1:6 in the upcoming *Grace Old Testament Commentary*:

> The knowledge that God has of the way of the righteous is experiential knowledge, and it shows that God approves and rewards those who are following Him. The second half of v 6 is antithetically parallel.
>
> The way of the wicked we might think would be unknown to the Lord considering the first line. But the psalmist says that his way shall perish. Perishing typically in the Bible refers to physical death. However, here it is not the sinner himself, but his way, that will perish.
>
> The point seems like that found in 1 Cor 3:10-15. Works without eternal value, that is, works that are like wood, hay, and straw, will burn up. They will perish. Only works with enduring value, works that are like gold, silver, and precious stones, will be rewarded. Church-age saints will be judged at the Bema. We do

---

[9] Warren Wiersbe, *Be Worshipful* (Colorado Springs, CO: Cook Communications Ministries, 2004), 15.

[10] Allen P. Ross, "Psalms," in *The Bible Knowledge Commentary*, eds. John F. Walvoord and Roy B. Zuck (Wheaton, IL: Victor Books, 1985), 791.

[11] Roger Ellsworth, *Opening up Psalms* (n.p: Day One Publications, 2006), 33.

> not know from Scripture the name of the judgment of OT believers.[12]

D. Ecclesiastes 12:13-14:

> Fear God and keep His commandments, for this is man's all. For God will bring every work into judgment, including every secret thing, whether good or bad.

Most commentators are vague about the judgment that Solomon has in mind. They repeat the words of the verse, but without indicating whether this is judgment in this life or after this life. Nor do they discuss whether those who "keep His commandments" include all believers or only faithful believers.

Glenn says that Solomon was talking about judgment in this life since "no evidence suggests that Solomon believed in such a judgment [after death]."[13]

Barnes takes the opposite position: "…an appointed judgment which shall take place in another world, as distinct from that retribution which frequently follows man's actions in the course of this world."[14]

Jamieson, Fausset, and Brown say that this refers to "future judgment,"[15] but they fail to explain their reasoning.

Simeon commented:

> If we have really had "the fear of God in our hearts," and "walked in his fear all the day long," and, under the influence of that principle, laboured to approve ourselves to him in all things, we shall assuredly hear him say to us in that day, "Well done, good and faithful servants, enter ye into the joy of your Lord."[16]

He does not say whether he understands Matt 25:21, which he quotes, to refer to eternal rewards or to eternal destiny. However, a bit

---

[12] Publication of *The Grace Old Testament Commentary* is scheduled for December of 2026.

[13] Don Glenn, "Ecclesiastes," in *The Bible Knowledge Commentary*, eds. John F. Walvoord and Roy B. Zuck (Wheaton, IL: Victor Books, 1985), 1006.

[14] Albert Barnes, *Notes on the Old Testament: Proverbs, Ecclesiastes, Song of Solomon, Jeremiah, Lamentations & Ezekiel* (London: John Murray, 1879), 113.

[15] Jamieson, Fausset, and Brown, *Commentary*, 414.

[16] Charles Simeon, *Horae Homileticae: Proverbs to Isaiah XXVI*, vol. 7 (London: Holdsworth and Ball, 1833), 417.

later he makes it clear that he has the latter in view: "holiness of heart and life is that which constitutes our meetness for heaven."[17]

Keil and Delitzsch say this refers to "certainty of a final judgment of personal character" and "the final judgment."[18]

In light of the teaching in both testaments of justification and regeneration by faith alone, apart from works, it is clear that this passage refers to judgment and recompense either in this life or in the life to come. Since Eccl 12:14 is a concluding statement and because of its use of the phrase "whether good or evil" (the same concept found in 2 Cor 5:10, part of a Bema passage), it is evident that this passage refers to eternal rewards for faithful service.

Here is what Brad Doskocil says in the upcoming *Grace Old Testament Commentary* about these key verses:

> **12:13.** After all the evidence has been examined, the conclusion is "fear God and keep His commandments…"
>
> **12:14.** The conclusion is universal in scope. God is going to judge every human work. Everyone's works will be evaluated by Jesus because He is the judge (John 5:22-23). The Bible presents two separate judgments of human works: one for believers who have everlasting life and another for unbelievers who are unregenerate.
>
> For believers, their judgment happens when Jesus returns to the earth to conquer it and establish His earthly kingdom (Matt 16:27, Luke 14:14, 2 Tim 2:12, Rev 2:26-27, 3:21, 20:4-6). This judgment is called the Judgment Seat of Christ (2 Cor 5:10). Jesus will evaluate every believer's works, whether good or bad, and reward him accordingly. These are eternal rewards which last forever. Jesus is fair. He compensates His workers for their service.
>
> The fact that both good and bad works are evaluated shows that believers are capable of doing good work and bad work in serving the Lord. Bad works are works that are not pleasing to the Lord or have

[17] Ibid., 419.

[18] Carl F. Keil and Franz Delitzsch, *Commentary on the Old Testament*, vol. 6 (Peabody, MA: Hendrickson, 1996), 816.

no value to Him. They will not be rewarded (1 Cor 3:13-15).

Secret works will be evaluated (Matt 6:1-24). These are works that no one else sees. They are not public. Yet, Jesus will not only know about them, but He will evaluate and reward them.[19]

IV. WHAT HEBREWS 11 TELLS US ABOUT REWARDS TEACHING IN THE OLD TESTAMENT

The author of Hebrews tells us that OT believers were motivated by eternal rewards. Here are some of the "OT Hall of Famers" highlighted in Hebrews 11 as being motivated by eternal rewards.

Enoch (Heb 11:5-6). Enoch "had this testimony, that he pleased God" (v 5). Then we read, "For without faith it is impossible to please Him, for he who comes to God must believe that He is, and that He is a rewarder of those who diligently seek Him." Enoch is an example of one who diligently sought God and will be rewarded by Him.

Moses (Heb 11:24-26). "By faith, Moses, when he became of age, refused to be called the son of Pharaoh's daughter, choosing rather to suffer affliction with the people of God than to enjoy the passing pleasures of sin, esteeming the reproach of Christ greater riches than the treasures in Egypt, *for he looked to the reward*" (emphasis added).

Sin has its temporary pleasures. But following Christ leads to lasting rewards. Moses knew this and eschewed the passing pleasures for the rewards to be received in the life to come.

Unnamed martyrs who lived before Christ's advent (Heb 11:35). "Women received their dead raised to life again. Others were tortured, not accepting deliverance, that they might obtain a better resurrection."

When I was new to the faculty of Multnomah, a chapel speaker quoted, without explanation, Heb 11:35. One of my students came up after chapel and asked me to explain the verse.

Anyone who knows John 3:16 knows that one does not gain everlasting life by persevering under torture to the point of death. The issue in Heb 11:35 is eternal rewards, not eternal destiny.

---

[19] Publication of *The Grace Old Testament Commentary* is scheduled for December of 2026.

Most commentators think this *better resurrection* is a resurrection better than the one experienced by "women [who] received their dead raised to life again" (v 36a). This probably refers to the two mothers whose sons Elijah and Elisha raised from the dead (1 Kgs 17:17-24; 2 Kgs 4:17-35). Wonderful as those miracles were, the women's sons eventually died again.

Jamison, Fausett, and Brown comment: "**a better resurrection**—than that of the women's children 'raised to life again'; or, than the resurrection which their foes could give them by delivering them from death (Dan 12:2; Luke 20:35; Phil 3:11)".[20]

Vincent agrees: "**A better resurrection** (κρείττονος ἀναστάσεως). Better than a resurrection like those granted to the women above mentioned, which gave merely a continuation of life on earth."[21]

However, others see the *better resurrection* as referring to eternal rewards.

Hodges comments: "[they] did so because they knew their sufferings would lead to a richer and better resurrection experience. So, the readers might also endure suffering staunchly and expect reward in the future world."[22]

Likewise, Tanner writes:

> Yet they were motivated by hopes of obtaining a better resurrection, not merely resuscitation. In this resurrection to come, they were consoled in knowing that God would reward them for having suffered for their faith.[23]

Hebrews 12:2 tells us that the Lord Himself was motivated to go to the cross by eternal rewards: "…looking unto Jesus, the author and finisher of our faith, *who for the joy that was set before Him* endured the cross, despising the shame, and has sat down at the right hand of the throne of God" (emphasis added).

Lea writes:

---

[20] Jamieson, Fausset, and Brown, *Commentary,* 474.

[21] Marvin R. Vincent, *Word Studies in the New Testament*, vol. 4 (Peabody, MA: Hendrickson Publishers, 1985), 533.

[22] Zane C. Hodges, "Hebrews," in *The Bible Knowledge Commentary*, eds. John F. Walvoord and Roy B. Zuck (Wheaton, IL: Victor Books, 1983), 809.

[23] J. Paul Tanner, "Hebrews," in *The Grace New Testament Commentary*, ed. Robert N. Wilkin (Denton, TX: Grace Evangelical Society, 2010), 1085.

> First, Jesus endured the cross to seize the blessed joy set before him. The path to victorious joy led through the cross. Second, Jesus scorned the shame of the cross. Jesus recognized the humiliation and ignominy of the cross, but these threats were of no consequence to him as he considered the coming glory. Third, Jesus sat down at the right hand of the throne of God. From the pain and agony of the cross God exalted Jesus to the position of a throne.[24]

There is a connection between this text and the many NT texts saying that if we persevere, we will rule with Christ and sit with Him on His throne (e.g., Rom 8:17-18; 1 Cor 9:24-27; 2 Tim 2:12; 4:17-19; Rev 2:26; 3:21).

V. WHAT THE FOUR GOSPELS TELL US ABOUT REWARDS TEACHING IN THE OLD TESTAMENT

I remember one of my OT professors, Dr. Allen Ross, telling me that the Gospels should be taught by the OT professors since they are OT literature. Though they were written after the birth of the church for people in the church age, they nonetheless report how OT people thought and acted.

When the Lord Jesus taught about eternal rewards, He was teaching OT people, not church age people.

A. The Parable of the Minas (Luke 19:11-27).

Here we have clear pre-church teaching that when Jesus returns, some will hear, "Well done, good servant," and be given rulership over ten cities (Luke 19:17). Some will not hear, "Well done," but yet will be given rulership over five cities (Luke 19:19). Others will be rebuked and will not receive any rulership, though they will get into the kingdom—in contrast to the unbelievers, who are slain (Luke 19:27).

Pate comments on v 27:

> Even though the action taken toward the disobedient servant was severe (even as it will be on Judgment Day

[24] Thomas D. Lea, *Hebrews & James* (Nashville, TN: Broadman & Holman Publishers, 1999), 219.

> for the unfaithful Christian), there is no hint in the text that the salvation of the faithless servant of the Lord was in jeopardy…The strong adversative (plēn) seems to contrast the punishment of the unprofitable servant with that of the master's enemies (cf. v. 14) who did not want him to rule over them."[25]

Morris, likewise, sees a distinction between the way in which Jesus deals with "his trading servants" and with "these enemies of mine."[26]

B. The Parable of the Just Servant and the Unjust Servant (Matthew 24:45-51).

Here, the Lord teaches OT people that if a believer who is doing well and is in line to rule in the life to come begins to think, "My Lord delays His coming," he might well fall out of fellowship with the Lord and forfeit the right to rule and reign. He will retain everlasting life, but not the reward of rulership.

However, many commentators think that the unjust servant is eternally condemned. Barbieri comments: "The judgment of the wicked at the Lord's second coming will separate them eternally from God."[27] France agrees, saying that the issue here is "ultimate salvation."[28]

The problem with that view is that it contradicts all the faith-alone promises in the Bible. Eternal destiny is based on faith in Christ, not faithfulness to Him.

Other examples of rewards teaching in the Gospels include the Parable of the Ten Virgins, the Parable of the Talents, the Judgment of the Sheep and the Goats, Matt 6:19-21 and 16:24-27 and their Synoptic parallels, and John 4:36 ("gathers fruit for eternal life").

VI. CONCLUSION

Believers before the birth of the Church knew a lot more about eternal rewards than we give them credit for.

The following OT believers believed in eternal rewards, according to Hebrews 11: Abel, Enoch, Noah, Abraham, Sarah, Isaac, Jacob, Joseph,

---

[25] C. Marvin Pate, *Luke* (Chicago, IL: Moody, 1995), 358.

[26] Leon Morris, *Luke*, rev. ed. (Grand Rapids, MI: Eerdmans, 1974, 1988), 302.

[27] Lou Barbieri, Jr., "Matthew," in *The Bible Knowledge Commentary*, eds. John F. Walvoord and Roy B. Zuck (Wheaton, IL: Victor Books, 1985), 79.

[28] R. T. France, *The Gospel of Matthew* (Grand Rapids, MI: Eerdmans, 2007), 946.

Moses, Joshua, Rahab, Gideon, Barak, Samson, Jephthah, Samuel, and David. Surely there were untold numbers of other OT believers who also believed in eternal rewards.

It is quite possible that a higher percentage of OT believers lived their lives in consideration of eternal rewards than do NT believers today.

Remember Gal 6:7: "...whatever a man sows, that he will also reap." That has always been true. Old Testament saints were guaranteed not only rewards in this life for work done, but rewards in the life to come, as well.

Have you ever considered that some of the choicest jobs in the kingdom will be taken by people who were either OT saints, such as King David, or OT saints who became NT saints, such as the eleven disciples and Matthias? David will be the Prince in the life to come. That job is already taken. The twelve apostles will sit on twelve thrones and rule over the twelve tribes of Israel. That means that they will be very close to the Lord Jesus. Those jobs are already taken.

Old Testament believers, like NT believers, will receive eternal rewards. And many OT saints knew about eternal rewards, just as many NT saints know about eternal rewards.

God has made us so that we are motivated in part by rewards. That is true in all aspects of life, including the Christian life. And it was also true of the life of OT believers, whether Jews or Gentiles.

BOOK REVIEWS

Receiving Back One's Deeds: A Protestant Reading of Justification and Final Judgment According to Works in 2 Corinthians. By Benjamin M. Dally. Lanham, MD: Lexington Books/Fortress Academic, 2023. 271 pp. Hardcover, $116.00.

I had never heard of Benjamin Dally until I came across this book, and I am not aware of any other books or articles he has published. The "about the author" page at the end of the book merely says that he holds a Ph.D. from Wheaton College and "serves as a church planter with Martus Collective in Wheaton, Illinois" (p. 273). According to the organization's website, this is "a ministry partner of Perception Funding" that helps "cross-cultural workers thrive in life and ministry." After conducting some research, I discovered that Dally also holds an M.Div. from Western Reformed Seminary and an M.A. in Biblical Exegesis from Wheaton, as well as an M.A. in Clinical Psychology. He is the founder and therapist of Kainos Counseling and Consultation, and has also served as an English, Youth, and Associate Pastor at a Wheaton Vietnamese C&MA Church. That being said, the book unexpectedly reads like the work of a theologian or seminary professor.

Receiving Back One's Deeds consists of an introduction and five chapters, the last of which is a "conclusion and synthesis." The book contains a bibliography that, though extensive, lists very few commentaries on Second Corinthians—which I see as a positive. Each chapter (including the introduction) contains endnotes, but so many as to be too many, especially the references to works in German. Overall, the book mirrors the footnotes in that it is somewhat wordy. The introduction is very detailed and includes a neat summary of each chapter. For the Biblical text, Dally utilizes the Nestle-Aland Greek text along with his own English translations. He accepts "the authenticity of all thirteen of the letters ascribed to Paul" (p. 8) and the unity of Second Corinthians.

The book investigates the relationship between justification by faith and judgment according to works and attempts to resolve the "theological tension" between "how one might be justified by faith alone and yet ultimately judged according to one's works" (p. 1). Dally maintains that "while not claiming to offer the final, definitive word on the matter, this study will attempt to demonstrate that the seeming tension between justification and final judgment can be alleviated while staying unwaveringly true to the fundamental pillars of the Reformation, *sola fide, sola gratia, solus Christus, sola Scriptura, soli Deo gloria*" (p.1).

In contrast to other investigations, Dally's study (1) delimits and illustrates "Protestant theological categories, positions, vocabulary, and modes of argument that will be drawn upon," (2) is a "focused examination of the meaning and rhetorical function of the 'judgment according to works' motif throughout Second Corinthians," and (3) makes use of "the category of 'narrative logic'" to understand "the ways that Paul's thought regarding the relationship between justification and judgment coheres and stands in continuity with the Scriptural traditions he has inherited and allowed to shape deeply his own theological convictions" (p. 2).

Dally argues a three-part thesis: (1) The believer's conduct "is best spoken of in the language of inferior/secondary 'cause' and/or 'basis' as far as its import at the last judgment"; (2) The believer's conduct "is soteriologically necessary [not solely, but secondarily nonetheless] and not simply of importance for the determination and/or bestowal of non-soteriological, eschatological rewards"; (3) There are crucial resources from the Protestant tradition to "authorize such ways of speaking" and "affirm these contentions in conjunction with a robust, strictly forensic/imputational, Reformational doctrine of justification by faith alone without restoring to the categories of 'paradox,' 'theological tension,' and the like to explain their coexistence" (p. 3).

The first chapter provides an excellent survey of the Reformation confessions of faith (Lutheran, Reformed, Anabaptist, and Anglican) as they pertain to the doctrine of justification and the role of works at the final judgment. Dally concludes that "no authoritative, Protestant consensus has ever existed regarding the nature of justification by faith or its relationship to final judgment according to works" (p. 49).

In chapter two, Dally introduces the reader to Early Jewish Restoration Theology (EJRT), which he defines as "any complex of beliefs concerning Israel's future maintained by Jews throughout the Second Temple period, particularly with regard to her eventual 'salvation' or 'deliverance' from her plight, that is, from the covenant curses promised at Sinai that had befallen her as a result of her unfaithfulness" (p. 95). He maintains that "the language and themes of EJRT are ubiquitous throughout 2 Cor 2:14–7:1" (p. 93).

The third chapter has two parts: (1) an examination of soteriology in Second Corinthians under the headings of predestination, faith, regeneration, covenant, assurance, and apostasy; and (2) an examination of the concept of justification in Second Corinthians.

The fourth chapter explores the topic of judgment according to works in Second Corinthians. Dally concludes that "at least at the exegetical level, that human conduct might legitimately be spoken of with the language of 'basis' and/or 'cause' (not solely or ultimately from a theological standpoint, but in a subordinate sense nonetheless) with regard to the determination of one's ultimate destiny, both for the believer and the unbeliever, due to the close, organic, and even in some sense causal relationship between one's conduct and divine judgment attested to in Paul's language" (p. 212).

The buildup to chapter five is palpable. It first offers a summary of the preceding chapters and then "a theological synthesis regarding the relationship between justification and judgment according to works" (p. 209). This synthesis consists of five observations of how Paul "takes up and reconfigures several aspects of EJRT" (p. 213), followed by five "propositional conclusions regarding the relationship between justification and judgment in Second Corinthians" (p. 213).

Dally's synthesis ultimately results in salvation by faith in Christ plus works: "It is not faith alone (in the confessional Lutheran sense) but divinely enabled, faith-fueled obedience that is of soteriological necessity at the final judgment" (p. 168); "one's conduct has implications for eternity" (p. 181); "those 'initiated into the process of salvation' can 'stand in danger of falling away'" (p. 182). Although Dally believes that justification is "through grace," "by faith alone," and "on account of the sacrificial death and resurrection of Christ alone, apart from any human merit," it is just a "forensic entryway" to salvation (pp. 215-16). It is merely "initial justification" (p. 218). "Final justification," which is "by faith alone and works," awaits the final judgment (p. 218). Although Christ's sacrifice, intercession, and atonement are "able to cover all past, present, and future sin," "perpetual forgiveness and cleansing from sin (cf. 1 John 1:8-9)" remain necessary (p. 217). Regarding the Judgment Seat of Christ in 2 Cor 5:10, which Dally considers "Paul's most explicit statement regarding judgment according to works"

(p. 170), he rejects the idea that Paul is speaking only of believers (p. 172) and rejects the idea of rewards (p. 173), which he equates with eternal life itself (pp. 177, 200).

According to Dally, one can be in Christ and in union with Christ with a new heart and then be severed from Christ and cast into hell. There is no eternal security. There is no assurance of salvation until the final judgment. The Judgment Seat of Christ is the same as the Great White Throne judgment. The conclusion is inescapable: The promises of salvation and eternal life (John 3:16, 36; 5:24; Acts 16:31; Rom. 4:5) by simply believing are not credible. Both faith and works are required. It is no surprise that Dally misapplies the OT Scriptures dealing with Israel to the Church. What is surprising, though, is that he never explicitly defines or describes the nature of the earthly conduct necessary for final salvation or the criteria by which such conduct is judged. Nor does he explain how "perpetual forgiveness and cleansing from sin" (p. 217) relate to this. Obedience and a righteous life in communion with God are necessary to make it through the last judgment, but "one's status as righteous in union with Christ may be forfeited and/or severed through perpetual, covenant-breaking disobedience, loss of faith, and apostasy" (p. 216).

I will give Dally credit for one thing. *Receiving Back One's Deeds* is the most exhaustive attempt I have ever seen to resolve the "theological tension" between "how one might be justified by faith alone and yet ultimately judged according to one's works" (p. 1). I can recommend the book only to believers who are grounded in the free grace of God and are interested in a thorough theological treatise on the subject or are undertaking a serious, in-depth study of 2 Corinthians. For the antidote to Dally's views, I would refer the reader to Robert Wilkin's contribution in *Four Views on the Role of Works at the Final Judgment* (Zondervan, 2013).

Laurence M. Vance
Vance Publications
Orlando, FL

Intermediate Greek Grammar: Syntax for Students of the New Testament. By David L. Mathewson and Elodie Ballantine Emig. Grand Rapids, MI: Baker Academic, 2016. 336 pp. Hardcover, $32.99.

This book is an exception to the dictum that New Testament Greek grammars are long-winded. It is only one inch thick, with few wasted words. The authors contrast their model with that of many others. In articulating their own approach, Mathewson and Emig say:

> As authors, we are committed to the authority and inspiration of Scripture. However this does not necessitate taking the Greek language in an unnatural or artificial way. Inspiration does not somehow transform the language into something more than it was before. Therefore we are committed to a minimalistic view of grammar, where maximal meaning is not attributed to the individual linguistic units but is found in their broader context. (pp. xviii-xix)

The book does not focus on grace issues. It does, however, offer solid advice on John 8:30-31. This is a passage non-grace people often twist.

One commonly accepted myth about Greek is that the present tense refers to actions that go on and on. Many have claimed that the present tense in 1 John 3:9 means that a believer cannot continue sinning. Most people who affirm that approach to the passage would also (rightly) deny that believers can attain sinless perfection in this life. That is double-speak in the Orwellian tradition.

Mathewson and Emig reject the habitual-sin approach to 1 John 3:

> …some have concluded that the present tense should be seen as indicating continuous, habitual, or repeated (iterative) action: Christians do not "continue in sin" or "habitually sin." The NIV reflects this interpretation: "No one who is born of God will continue to sin…" See also the NIV's translation of 3:6b ("No one who continues to sin…"). However, this is a misunderstanding of the present tense and illegitimately attributes a continuous notion or repetition to the present without clear contextual clues. The present tense only looks at the action as a process in progress. More likely, 1 John 3:9 is just a general reference (that

> person "does not sin"), with no indication of duration or repetition. (p. 130)

The final sentence of the above citation leaves many questions unanswered. Although Mathewson and Emig do not explain all the pertinent issues in 1 John 3:6, 9, they are helpful. Minimalist grammar strives to avoid eisegetical overstatement.

I do appreciate their desire to avoid over-refinement. However, one must be aware that Mathewson and Emig focus on more commonly addressed categories. Their listings, therefore, are not always exhaustive. Here is their listing of the genitive:

[1] Genitive Constructions Restricting Substantives [12-19]
- [A] Descriptive (attributive, qualitative) [12-13]
- [B] Possessive and source (relationship, origin) [13-14]
- [C] Subjective and objective [14-17]
- [D] Epexegetical/appositional [17-18]
- [E] Partitive [18-19]

[2] Genitive Constructions Restricting Adjectives or Verbs [19-21]
- [A] With adjectives (and occasionally adverbs) [19-20]
- [B] With verbs [20-21]
    1. Genitive expressing time [20]
    2. Genitive expressing price [21]
- [C] As objects of verbs [21]
- [D] Genitive absolute [21]

Wallace lists all the categories that Mathewson and Emig do. However, they omit a number of legitimate categories that Wallace includes. Although Mathewson and Emig discuss the most frequent usages, other (unmentioned) categories do legitimately exist.

In defense of Mathewson and Emig, their desire to avoid over refinement prevented them from including two of Wallace's wrong-headed categories: the genitive of subordination and the plenary genitive.

The genitive of subordination is an unnecessary subcategory of the objective genitive. Nothing is gained by creating this classification. Likewise, the plenary genitive is a case of wanting *and* when *or* is sufficient.

This illustrates a general difference of Mathewson and Emig versus Wallace. While Mathewson and Emig should be praised for resisting the unnecessary multiplication of categories, their deficiency is that in doing so, they leave a number of legitimate categories unmentioned.

I am now a retired professor. Were I still teaching, I would likely utilize both grammars mentioned in this review. My courses were always heavy on grammatical diagramming. The questions that diagrams require students to answer would sort out issues between these grammars. For common categories, Mathewson and Emig usually provide enough information to enable students to successfully complete a diagram. When students encounter situations lying outside Mathewson and Emig's discussions, they should consult Wallace. If they are still unable to complete the diagram satisfactorily, classroom discussion (moderated by the professor) would guide everyone toward grammatical clarity.

I would like to see a 100-page expansion of Mathewson and Emig in a second edition. This would not create a long-winded grammar, but would extend their minimalist approach to include other legitimate categories that exegetes can and do encounter.

They also need to provide more complete tables of contents. Wallace's tables of contents offer a refreshing level of transparency. Mathewson and Emig make it much more difficult to discern how completely they do or don't handle topics.

I recommend this work but see room for improvement in a second edition.

John H. Niemelä
Message of Life
Knoxville, TN

John 1:1–7:1. By William C. Weinrich. Concordia Commentary, ed. Curtis P. Geise. St. Louis, MO: Concordia, 2015. 863 pp. Hardback. $64.99.

John 7:2–12:50. By William C. Weinrich. Concordia Commentary, ed. Curtis P. Geise. St. Louis, MO: Concordia, 2022. 867 pp. Hardback. $64.99.

Like most Finns, my upbringing was Lutheran. I do check out their commentaries because, on certain issues, Lutherans critique both Arminians and Calvinists. This does not imply that they regard assurance as of the essence of saving faith. Additionally, few Lutherans, after George N. H. Peters (1825–1909), have been dispensational.

Lutherans often fixate on a sacramental understanding of baptism and communion.[1] Thus, even a section starting with decent exposition may suddenly digress into sacramentalism.

Weinrich is a mixed bag. Positively, he (like Luther) opposes Augustine's notion that only the elect are drawn in John 6:44: *No one can come to Me unless the Father who sent Me draws him…*

Weinrich cites favorably Luther's gentle approach to drawing:

> When God draws us, He is not like a hangman, who drags a thief up the ladder to the gallows; but He allures and coaxes us in a friendly fashion, as a kind man attracts people by his amiability and cordiality, and everyone willingly goes to him. Thus God, too, gently draws people to Himself, so that they abide with him willingly and happily...Then you hear that God is not hostile to you, but is your gracious and merciful Father, who gave His Son for you, let Him die for you, and raised Him again from the dead. He directs you to the Son and has proclaimed Him to you. And if this is correctly taught, then we come to him. That is meant by the expression "to be drawn" [Jn 6:44].[2]

This is a sharp contrast to the view of Augustine or Calvin, which is overbearing (to put it kindly).

Another positive is that Weinrich swims against the current in dating John's Gospel. He devotes fourteen pages (1:31-44) to eight pet arguments of late-daters. Then (1:44-51) he makes a positive case for a fairly early date. He concludes, "I would propose that the Gospel of John was composed in Jerusalem during the 40s and taken with John to Asia Minor in the early 50s" [1:51]. This reviewer dates John even earlier (before AD 44; i.e., before Cornelius and the inclusion of Gentiles in Acts 10), but this section of Weinrich is refreshing.

Some may ask, "So what?" The notion that God would wait until the 60s or even the 90s to inspire the only NT book addressing unbelievers seems odd. Weinrich fails to mention John 21:24 as key

---

[1] Lutherans rightly dismiss five of Catholicism's seven sacraments, but cling to relics by insisting on a sacramentarian understanding of baptism and communion.

[2] Weinrich, *John*, 1:714-15, quoting Martin Luther, "Tenth Sermon on John 6," in *Luther's Works*, American Edition, vol. 23 (St. Louis, MO: Concordia, 1958), 714-15.

evidence for an early date: Other apostles were alive when John wrote his Gospel.[3]

Weinrich does not follow the crowd regarding John 8:33, although the word *certainly* would be far better than his *perhaps*: "Although those who now respond [negatively] may seem to be the believing Jews mentioned in Jn. 8:31, perhaps this response and the subsequent dialogue come from another group of Jews who have been and remain hostile to Jesus."[4]

One might imagine that Weinrich's early date for John's Gospel would lead him to let John's Gospel speak for itself on topics like baptism. No, not at all! His understanding of *water* is—one might say—all wet. Volume 1 discusses baptism (of Jesus, of people by John, of people by Jesus with water, and of people by Jesus with the Spirit) on 153 pages, while volume 2 considers it on sixty-four pages. That is 217 pages for a word, *baptizō* (baptize), that occurs only thirteen times in eleven of John's 879 verses. The same sections use *pisteuō* (believe) thirty-eight times, but volumes 1–2 discuss *belief*, *faith*, *trust*, and *unbelief* (words related to *pisteuō*) on 178 pages. How is it that *pisteuō*, the key term of the book, receives significantly less attention than *baptizō*, a minor term? This amounts to majoring in the minors.

Weinrich does not even make a pretense of adhering to *sola fide* (faith alone). Besides advocating replacement theology, he gratuitously adds baptism to the gospel's purpose statement (John 20:30-31):

> The Gospel of John thus invites the reader/hearer to participate in the new exodus which lies in **the Sacrament of Baptism**...We might, therefore, paraphrase the purpose statement of John's Gospel in the following manner:
>
>> Many signs were done by Jesus in the sight of his disciples. These signs were written in this Torah book of the new Israel[5] in order that you,

---

[3] First person plurals (*we*, *our*, *us*) in John's editorial parentheses refer to the Eleven. Compare John 1:14 with 1 John 1:1-5. In keeping with that pattern, understanding *we* in John 21:24 as the apostles is not only the expected sense, but the one that agrees with John 20:30-31, the purpose statement: "Thus Jesus did many other signs in the sight of His disciples [us], which have not been written in this book. But these *signs* [that we have witnessed] have been written..."

[4] Weinrich, *John*, 2:128. That is, he is open to the possibility that the speakers in John 8:33 were not the new believers (John 8:30-31). See John H. Niemelä, "Free at Last! Freedom in Jesus' Footsteps (John 8:30-32)," *JOTGES* 31 (Autumn 2018): 57-72.

[5] He would see the church (the new Israel) replacing Israel. This would abrogate God's

> O Jew of the synagogue, might become firmly convinced that Jesus is the Anointed One, the Son of God. As the Anointed One, Jesus is he who possesses the Spirit and will give over the Spirit, and as the Son of God, Jesus is he through whom and in whom one may become a child of God. **This Gospel is thus written in order that you might so believe, and so believing you might be baptized in his Name and thereby receive eternal life**[6] [emphasis added].

> The ongoing and repeated use of the image of water [in John] is not merely symbolic for revelation or some other heavenly gift. The reality of water is given first in the baptism of John, and it is the water of this baptism which through the work of Christ, is transformed by the way of the Spirit into the 'living water" of John 4. Between John the Baptist and Jesus there is continuity, but there is also advance: John baptized with water, but Jesus baptizes with water and with the Spirit (Jn. 1:33; 3:3, 5).[7]

About the only time water does not trigger an association with baptism for Weinrich is when John mentions the Sea of Galilee. Volume 1 mentions baptism/baptized/Jesus' baptism on 153 of 776 (i.e., 20%) text pages. He even devotes eighteen pages to: "Does John 9 [the blind man washing at Siloam] refer to Baptism?"[8] Weinrich imagines that the passage actually refers to baptism.[9]

The 153 pages in volume 1 that refer to baptism fall into sixty clusters. In John 1:1–7:1, the focus of volume 1, the word "*baptize*" occurs twelve times (1:25-26, 28, 31, 33ab; 3:22, 23ab, 26; 4:1-2). These form three categories:

1. John baptizing people with water: 1:25-26, 28, 31, 33a; 3:23ab; 10:40;

unconditional promissory covenants with Israel (the Abrahamic, Land, Davidic, and New Covenants).

6 Weinrich, *John*, 1:13-14.

7 Weinrich, *John*, 1:250-51.

8 Weinrich, *John*, 2:318-35.

9 Weinrich, *John*, 2:335.

2. Jesus/His disciples baptizing people with water: 3:22, 26; 4:1-2;
3. Jesus predicted to baptize with the Spirit: 1:33b.

Not a single passage in John's Gospel even alludes to John baptizing Jesus.[10]

Not surprisingly, the purpose statement of John eludes Weinrich. He twists a faith-alone message into baptismal regeneration.

This commentary was a huge disappointment. I expected a sacramentarian emphasis. I expected a church history professor to be overly impressed with post-NT writers. I expected a faith-plus message. But his handling of the date of writing seemed to promise a willingness to engage the text and follow the evidence. On issues that are not Lutheran distinctives, he can offer some insights. Unfortunately, one must wade through nearly 2,000 pages to find them.

Weinrich is familiar with a vast swath of the literature on John. Not surprisingly, he often cites Patristic writers and Luther's voluminous works, more so than any other commentary on John that I possess. Since I prioritize the text over theologians of prior centuries, he saves me time in finding scattered ancient tidbits. These overpriced volumes push a theological agenda. I do not recommend them for any but the most discerning readers.

John H. Niemelä
Message of Life
Knoxville, TN

No God but One: A Former Muslim Investigates the Evidence for Islam and Christianity. By Nabeel Qureshi. Grand Rapids, MI: Zondervan, 2016. 316 pp. Paper, $17.99.

Seeking Allah, Finding Jesus. By Nabeel Qureshi. Grand Rapids, MI: Zondervan, 2014 (expanded, 2016). 363 pp. Paper, $17.99.

You might say, "I can't think of a reason to delve into the details of Islam, so why would I want these books?" That was also my thought

---

[10] Weinrich, *John*, 1:237, rightly recognizes this: "…the Baptism of Jesus is not explicitly recorded at all [in John]; it is rather assumed as having already happened." Many assume that the baptism of Jesus occurred on the first day that the Baptist said, "Behold, the Lamb of God." If so, one would need to reconcile the series of days in John that follow 1:29 (1:35, 43) with Mark's account. Mark 1:12 says, "Immediately [after Jesus' baptism] the Spirit drove Him into the wilderness [to be tempted]." Chronology requires concluding that Jesus' baptism occurred prior to the point at which John's narrative picks up.

until Dix Winston used an illustration from Nabeel Qureshi's *No God but One*. Qureshi was in Oakland, CA, for an eight-week Arabic-language immersion course. A friend introduced him to a woman named Sahar. Her question centered on a major obstacle for Muslims regarding Christianity: "How can you believe Jesus is God if He was born through the birth canal of a woman and He had to use the bathroom? Aren't these things below God?" (*NGBO*, p. 89).

After saying that he understood her concern, Qureshi asked, "Sahar, let's imagine that you are on your way to a very important ceremony and are dressed in your finest clothes. You're about to arrive just in time, but then you see your daughter drowning in a pool of mud. What would you do? Let her drown and arrive looking dignified, or rescue her and arrive at the ceremony covered in mud?" (p. 91). Later that week, Nabeel's friend invited him to meet a new convert from Islam. It was Sahar.

Thinking that Nabeel Qureshi might have some pertinent things to say on other hot-button issues, I bought the book. Muslims believe in the absolute oneness of God. They reject the Trinity as tri-theism. They are not alone. Jehovah's Witnesses—as well as Jews who take the *Ta̱na̱kh* (the Old Testament) seriously—see this as a deal-breaker. Jesus often needed to dismantle charges of blasphemy. I think Qureshi explains things simply and effectively. For example:

> Christianity has always taught there is only one God. Where Christian theology differs from other forms of monotheism is not on the number of gods, but on the concept of God's personhood. The doctrine of the Trinity teaches that one God exists as three persons.
>
> It is at this point that Muslims often level a charge of self-contradiction, but it certainly is not, and here is why: *person* is not the same as *being*. Your being is the quality that makes you *what* you are, but your person is the quality that makes you *who* you are. For example, we are humans. That is *what* we are. That is why we are called human *beings*. But *what* we are is not the same as *who* we are. If someone asks, "Who are you?" I should not respond by saying, "A human!" That answers the question of what I am not who I am. Who I am is Nabeel; that is my person. What I am

> is a human; that is my being. Being and person are separate.
>
> Unlike a human being, which has only one person, God has three persons. He is one being, Yahweh, in three persons: Father, Son and Spirit. He's more than able to exist like that because he is God. If we say God must have only one person like humans, then we are making God in our image. Who are we to limit God? It is up to God to tell us who he is. (*NGBO*, p. 56)

During Qureshi's four years (2001–05) at Old Dominion University, he and classmate David Wood had a continuing dialogue regarding the Quran versus the Bible. Early in their friendship, David and Nabeel studied the Bible, the Quran, the Hadith, and other pertinent writings in order to determine the truth/falsity of the following five issues:

1. Jesus' death by crucifixion
2. Jesus' resurrection from the dead
3. Jesus' claim to be God
4. The prophetic authority of Muhammad
5. The divine inspiration of the Quran (*NGBO*, p. 155)

The first three issues make or break the case for Christianity; the final two do so for Islam. *No God but One* examines the relevant writings in a point/counterpoint manner to help Muslims become more receptive to Christianity and to clarify issues for Christians. The second book, *Seeking Allah, Finding Jesus*, traces the narrative of discussions and events over four years that led Qureshi to embrace Christianity.

Sadly, Qureshi died from stomach cancer at age thirty-four. At the time, he was an apologist with Ravi Zacharias International Ministries. His educational credentials are impressive:

> B.A. Old Dominion University
> M.A. Biola University (Christian theology)
> M.D. Eastern Virginia Medical School
> M.A. Duke University (Christianity and Islam)
> M.Phil. University of Oxford (Judaism and Christianity)
> Studies toward a D.Phil. at Oxford (interrupted by death)

Unfortunately, Qureshi does not present a clear faith-alone-in-Jesus-Christ-alone message. Three references demonstrate that—in addition to a lack of clarity—he presents a moving-target message:

> For Christianity, we [David Woods and Nabeel] found the answer [Christianity's central tenets] in Romans 10:9: "If you declare with your mouth, 'Jesus is Lord,' and believe in your heart that God raised him from the dead, you will be saved" (NIV). Here we found the entire gospel message formulated as the minimum requirement for saving faith. It has three components: (1) that Jesus died, (2) that he rose from the dead, and (3) that he is God. (*NGBO*, pp. 152-53)
>
> Those of us who wish to accept God's sacrifice on our behalf must repent of our sins and yield ourselves to following him. (*NGBO*, p. 36)
>
> I submit. I submit that Jesus Christ is Lord of heaven and earth. He came to this world to die for my sins, proving his lordship by rising from the dead. I am a sinner and I need him for redemption. Christ, I accept you into my life. (*SAFJ*, pp. 278-79)

Is it faith? Is it confession? Is it repentance? Is it yielding? Is it submission? Is it accepting Jesus into one's life? With regard to believing, he has three content items but never states the core message—that Jesus irrevocably guarantees everlasting life to those who believe Him for that promise.

Obviously, these three citations are problematic, but neither book dwells on defining the message that gives life. In these books, that is a positive, because they focus on areas where Qureshi is clear: The case for Christianity stands; the case for Islam does not. Thankfully, the confusion evident in the three cited paragraphs is largely limited to those paragraphs.

I reject Qureshi's preference for the critical text (*SAFJ*, pp. 130-33; 304-08), but salute him for maintaining that the original text is recoverable via sound textual criticism. The Muslim allegation is that the NT has been hopelessly corrupted to the point that no one can discern the original. His presentation of the corruption of the Quranic text (*NGBO*, pp. 281-83; and *SAFJ*, pp. 236-41) is fascinating.

I recommend these books. Certainly, it would have been preferable had Qureshi either advocated Jesus' message of life, or simply left a few things unsaid. Still, the books can be helpful in thinking through issues for ministry to Muslims, religious Jews, Jehovah's Witnesses, and anyone who imagines that Christians worship three gods.

John H. Niemelä
Message of Life
Knoxville, TN

Made in the USA
Coppell, TX
20 December 2025

65260480R00066